pen rhythms

Poetry for GCSE and Standard Grade

Chris Webster

Advisory Teacher for English, Hertfordshire

Stanley Thornes (Publishers) Ltd

Contents

Pen Rhythms

Pen rhythms
Rhyme patterns
Thought shapes
Sound-scapes
Sound patterns
Rhyme shapes
Thought rhythms
Pen-scapes
Thought patterns
Pen shapes
Rhyme-scapes
Sound rhythms
Sound shapes
Thought-scapes
Rhyme rhythms
Pen patterns:
    POETRY!

Acknowledgements

I would like to thank all the pupils at The Appleton School, South Benfleet who worked through the Mark One version of this book, and who contributed many more good poems than could be reproduced here. I would also like to thank my wife, Julie, for her encouragement, and my children, Melanie, Nicholas and Charlotte, for trying to behave themselves while I was in the loft writing this.

Chris Webster

The author and publishers are grateful to the following for permission to reproduce poems, extracts and other text materials:

Allen Brady & Marsh Ltd for the Midland Bank Personal Loan advertisement, page 3 • Ambit for 'Snooker Player' by Richard Freeman, *Ambit*, 1973, page 73 • Angus & Robertson (UK) Ltd for 'Snake Glides' from *And I Dance* by Keith Bosley, page 148; 'Lit-elle messe, moffette' and 'Chacun Gille' from *Mots d'Heures: Gousses, Rames: The d'Antin Manuscript* edited and annotated by Luis d'Antin Van Rooten, 1968; page 30 • Anvil Press Poetry Ltd for 'Dirge' by Gavin Bantock from *A New Thing Breathing*, 1969, page 35 • Autolycus Press and Hubert Nicholson for 'The Ad-Man' by A S J Tessimond from *The Collected Poems of A S J Tessimond*, page 53 • BBC Enterprises for the street rap by Perry P from *The Story of the English* by Robert McCrum *et al*, page 17 • James Bernard, Executor of the Literary Estate of Paul Dehn, for 'Gutter Press' from *The Fern on the Rock* by Paul Dehn, page 55 • A & C Black (Publishers) Ltd for 'From the Rain-Making Ceremony' by J H Driberg, page 22 • Book Tokens Ltd for a book token advertisement, page 46 • Alan Brownjohn for 'Common Sense', page 150 • Jonathan Cape Ltd for 'To Whom it May Concern' from *Out Loud* by Adrian Mitchell, Cape Goliard Press, page 42; 'The Commission', 'Goodbat Nightman' and 'The Future' from *In The Glassroom*, 'the power of poets' from *Gig* and 'If Life's a Lousy Picture, Why Not Leave Before the End' from *Watchwords* by Roger McGough, pages 77, 95, 147, 9, 71; and on behalf of the Executors of the Estate of C Day Lewis for 'The Ecstatic' from *Collected Poems: 1954* by C Day Lewis, The Hogarth Press, page 14 • Carcanet Press Ltd for 'Opening the Cage' from *Poems of 30 Years* by Edwin Morgan, page 9 • Carlin Music Corporation for 'Sunrise, Sunset' by Sheldon Harnick, page 5 • Cassell plc for 'Lark' by George Macbeth from *Words 3*, page 13 • Laura Cecil on behalf of The James Reeves Estate for 'The Song of the Dumb Waiter' by James Reeves from *James Reeves: The Complete Poems for Children*, Heinemann, © James Reeves, page 92 • Chappell Music Ltd for 'Imagine' by John Winston Lennon, © 1971 MacLen Music Incorporated, page 38 • Chatto & Windus Ltd for 'A Poem is' from *The Anzac Sonata* and 'A Poem about Poems about Vietnam' by Jon Stallworthy, pages 15, 43; 'Cold Song' from *The White Bird* by Norman MacCaig, page 35; 'Old Movies' from *Old Movies* by John Cotton, page 125; and 'The Last Laugh' from *Collected Poems of Wilfred Owen* edited by C Day Lewis, page 103 • Andre Deutsch Ltd for 'Tonight at Noon' from *Tonight at Noon* by Adrian Henri, page 134; and 'Mirror' by John Updike, page 144 • Dolphin Concert Productions Ltd for 'Rocking Gran Blues' by Pam Ayres, © Pam Ayres, page 66 • Echo Newspapers for extracts from various issues of the *Standard Recorder*; page 94 • English Folk Dance and Song Society for 'Salisbury Plain', page 21 • Ess-Food Danepak Ltd for a bacon advertisement, page 29 • Faber and Faber Ltd for 'Elvis Presley' from *The Sense of Movement* by Thom Gunn, page 67; 'The Express' from *Collected Poems* by Stephen Spender, page 102; 'Beware of the Stars' from *Moortown* and 'The Vampire' from *The Hawk in the Rain* by Ted Hughes, pages 39, 79 • Alan Gilbey for 'Disruptive minority', page 112 • Grafton Books for 'Nothing' from *Complete Poems 1913-62* by e e cummings, page 10 • Grove Press, Inc. for 'Fond Farewell to the Chicago Review' by Philip Whalen, *Evergreen Review*, Summer 1959, © 1959 by Evergreen Review, Inc., page 140 • Harcourt Brace Jovanovich, Inc. for 'Money' from *The People, Yes*, by Carl Sandburg, © 1936 Harcourt Brace Jovanovich, Inc. renewed 1964 by Carl Sandburg, page 77 • Jean Henderson for 'Badger' by John Tripp, page 118 • David Higham Associates Ltd on behalf of the authors for 'Poetry Today' from *The Blue-Fly in his Head* by John Heath-Stubbs, Oxford University Press, 1962, page 132; and 'Windscale' from *A Local Habitation* by Norman Nicholson, page 116 • Philip Hobsbaum for 'Girl Reporter', page 54 • Michael Horovitz for 'Sea's Cape' from *Growing Up*, page 93 • Illegal Music Ltd for 'Every Breath You Take' by Sting, page 34 • International Laboratories Ltd for a Wasp-eze advertisement, page 2 • James Kirkup for 'A London Spring', page 50 • London Express News and Feature Services for an extract from issue, 22.4.86, *The Star*, page 100 • London Magazine Editions for 'Splendid Girls' by John Normanton from *London Magazine Poems 1961-6*, page 124 • Longman Group Ltd for 270 'Ship' entry from *Roget's Thesaurus*, page 81 • Jennifer Luithlen Agency on behalf of the author for 'Ned Nott' and 'There's no need to light . . .' from *The World's Toughest Tongue Twisters* by R Rosenbloom, Ravette Ltd, page 31 • Macmillan Publishers Ltd for 'Breakfast' from *Collected Poems 1905-25* by W W Gibson, page 39 • Adam McNaughton for 'Oor Hamlet' from *Across the Clyde*, Puffin Books, page 24 • The Marvell Press for 'Reasons for Attendance' from *The Less Deceived* by Philip Larkin, page 64 • Spike Milligan Productions Ltd for 'An Ear passed me' from *The Bedside Milligan* by Spike Milligan, 1983, page 93 • John Murray (Publishers) Ltd for 'Executive' from *Collected Poems* by John Betjeman, page 87 • New Directions Publishing Corporation for 'Constantly risking absurdity' from *A Coney Island of the Mind* by Lawrence Ferlinghetti, © 1958 Lawrence Ferlinghetti, page 139 • NSPCC for child neglect advertisement, page 74 • Octopus Publishing Group plc for skylark entry from *A Colour Guide to Familiar Garden and Field Birds* by Jiri Felix, page 11 • Oval Music Ltd for '19' by Paul Hardcastle, Jonas McCord and William Couturie © 1985 Oval Music Ltd, page 40 • Oxford University Press for 'Benediction' from *Chain of Days* by James Berry, 1985, page 6; 'Foodless Children' by Maldwyn Davies and 'Assault' by Erno Muller from *Every Man Will Shout* edited by Roger Mansfield and Isobel Armstrong, 1964, © 1964 Oxford University Press, pages 117, 119 • Pan Books Ltd for material from *A Small Book of Grave Humour* by Fritz Spiegl, page 7 • Penguin Books Ltd for 'Busy Day' by Michael Rosen from *You Tell Me* by Roger McGough and Michael Rosen and associated illustrations by Sara Midden, Kestrel Books, © 1979 Michael Rosen and Sara Midden, page 138; extract from *Beowulf* translated by Michael Alexander, Penguin Classics, © 1973 Michael Alexander, page 18; 'Zion, me wan go home' from *The Penguin Book of Caribbean Verse* edited by Paula Burnett, Collection © 1986 Paula Burnett, page 37; 'Two Anglo-Saxon Riddles' and 'From the Battle of Maldon' from *The Earliest English Poems* translated by Michael Alexander, Penguin Classics, © 1966, 1977 Michael Alexander, page 97; 'The Grave of Little Su' by Li Ho and 'Farewell Poem' by Lu Mu from *Poems of the Late T'Ang* translated by A C Graham, Penguin Classics, © 1965 A C Graham, pages 110, 127 • A D Peters & Co. Ltd on behalf of the author for extract from 'summer with monika' from *Frink* by Roger McGough, page 136 • Pifco Salton Ltd for vacuum bag sealer advertisement, page 38 • Polygram Music Publishing for 'Candle in the Wind' by Elton John and Bernie Taupin, Dick James Music Ltd, page 123 • Deborah Rogers Ltd on behalf of the author for 'The New, Fast, Automated Daffodils' from *Collected Poems* by Adrian Henri, © 1986 Adrian Henri, page 143 • Roland Rat Enterprises Ltd for 'Rat Rapping' by Roland Rat/Stephen Jeffries, page 28 • Routledge and Kegan Paul for 'William Wordsworth' from *Collected Poems* by Sidney Keyes, page 164 • Rowntree Mackintosh Confectionery Ltd for a chocolate advertisement, page 4 • George Sasson for 'Base Details' by Siegfried Sassoon, page 120 • Vernon Scannell for 'A Case of Murder', page 107 • Shire Productions Ltd for material from *Discovering Epitaphs* by G Wright, page 7 • James Simmons for 'Kill the Children', page 111 • The Society of Authors on behalf of the Estate of John Masefield for 'Cargoes' by John Masefield, page 82 • Solo Syndication & Literary Agency Ltd for an extract from issue 21.8.85, *Daily Mail*, page 94 • Mary Ellen Solt for 'Marriage', design by Mary Ellen Solt, drawing by Sheryl Nelson, The Finial Press; 'Fosythia', design by Mary Ellen Solt, typography by John Dearstyne and 'Moonshot Sonnet', design by Mary Ellen Solt, drawing by Timothy Mayer from *Concrete Poetry: A World Apart* edited by Mary Ellen Solt, pages 145, 146, 155 • John O Thompson for '35 feet deep in the wet language', page 127 • D C Thompson & Co. Ltd for extract from issue 24.10.87, *Jackie*, © 1987 D C Thompson & Co. Ltd, page 152 • Unwin Hyman Ltd for 'Where Are You Now Superman?' and 'Prose Poem towards a Definition of Itself' from *Little Johnny's Confession* by Brian Patten, pages 137, 153 • Warner Bros Music Ltd for 'The Rose' by Amanda McBroom, © 20th Century Music Corp./Hollywood Allstar Music, page 126 • David Watkin Price for 'Kite', page 148 • A P Watt Ltd on behalf of The Executors of the Estate of Robert Graves for 'Tilth' from *Collected Poems 1975* by Robert Graves, page 88 •

We are also grateful to the following for permission to reproduce photographs:

Associated Press, page 42 • Atomic Energy Authority, page 116 • Barnaby's Picture Library, pages 13, 27, 39, 49, 64, 75, 76, 86, 101, 102, 109, 111, 140, 142, 152 • BBC Hulton Picture Library, pages 21, 25, 26, 62, 72, 83, 117, 119, 122 • Robert Cottingham, page 125 • Janet Gill/Lloyd's of London, page 33 • Kunsthalle, Tübingen, page 136 • RCA, page 67 • Roland Rat Enterprises, page 28 • Sting (photo by Brian Aris), page 34 • Tate Gallery, London, page 135.

Every effort has been made to contact copyright holders, and we apologise if any have been overlooked.

1 Discovering Poetry

Poetry is a way of taking life by the throat.

Robert Frost

This book was written in the belief that poetry is so important that no one should miss out on it.

It is important because:

- it can help you make sense of life – it deals with things we all experience, or might experience: growing up, falling in love, coping with other people, perhaps even going to war.

- it is hard-hitting – it has a powerful voice on important issues. For example, one of the most powerful protests about war may be found in poetry.

- it can give pleasure – a poet's perceptive description can increase your own awareness and enjoyment of the things around you. There is also an aesthetic pleasure in the form, pattern and sound of a poem.

- it can sharpen your awareness of words – everyday carelessness can leave words 'shabby, worn, diminished, mean'. Poetry refreshes words with precise and creative usage.

- it can make you a better person – more than any other medium, poetry can take you into other people's lives and feelings, making you a more humane and understanding person.

How does poetry manage to do so much? That is one of the things this book will help you to find out, and since poetry is a part of everyday life, that is where we will start.

Poetry is everywhere, from your cereal packet to your birthday card. You probably read examples like these a dozen times a day and do not even know it:

1

This card is for your birthday,
A special day for you
To wish you all the very best,
And hope your dreams come true,
And most of all to let you know
You're very special too!

This bag is bright and gay
I hope you use it every day
But please remember it's not a toy
For play by little girl or boy
The Jolly Giant says
KEEP BAGS AWAY FROM INFANTS

THE THINGS PEOPLE BUY WITH MIDLAND PERSONAL LOANS

A VERY OLD SUIT...

...A CAR THAT'S A HOOT...

...AN ANTIQUE TIMER...

...A GRAND TOUR FOR MOTHER...

...A GIFT FOR A LOVER...

Even a visit to the school toilets could be a poetic experience – especially if there is some of the better quality graffiti to read:

3

Occasionally, you will come across something that goes much further than these simple rhymes, like this advertisement for After Eight mints:

HILARY HOBBS

who gobbled her After Eights and wasn't invited again.

HILARY HOBBS was the fashionable face,
 At parties and premières all over the place.
Though often asked to "drop in for a bite,"
 She seldom received a second invite.

For you see, she had this terrible habit,
 When offered an After Eight, she'd grab it,
And munch the elegant mint in one,
 A thing that is really never done.

Two bites at least, and four at most,
 Should satisfy even the strictest host.
Now that is why, and it's sad to say,
 She dines at home or takes away,

So be warned by Hilary Hobbs's fate,
 And never rush your After Eight.

or this song lyric:

SUNRISE, SUNSET

Is this the litle girl I carried?
Is this the little boy at play?
I don't remember growing older,
When did they?

When did she get to be a beauty?
When did he grow to be so tall?
Wasn't it yesterday when they were so small?

Now is the little boy a bridegroom,
Now is the little girl a bride.
Under the canopy I see them,
Side by side.

Place the gold ring around her finger,
Share the sweet wine and break the glass;
Soon the full circle will have come to pass.

Sunrise, sunset,
Sunrise sunset,
Swiftly flow the days;
Seedlings turn overnight to sunflowers,
Blossoming even as we gaze.

Sunrise, sunset,
Sunrise, sunset,
Swiftly fly the years;
One season following another,
Laden with happiness and tears.
Happiness and tears.

Sheldom Harnick

These everyday examples use a range of poetic techniques including rhyme, alliteration,
wordplay and line layout. Notice, for example, how effectively rhyme hammers home
the need for a pain-relief spray or the brand-name of a chocolate mint. Of course, most
of these examples are not poetry in the full sense of the word because they are so

trivial (there are more important things in life than chocolate mints!) and because the advertiser's main aim is to sell, whereas poets are concerned only with the truth. However, they do show the effectiveness of some of the main poetic techniques.

How much more effective these techniques are when used by a good poet for a worthwhile end can be seen in the poem below by James Berry, which is a part of everyday life for London commuters (it is one of a series of poster poems designed for use on the Underground). His simple, yet powerful appreciation of human senses makes a refreshing contrast to the blatant salesmanship of the advertisements that surround it.

Poems on the Underground

BENEDICTION

❧

James Berry

1924-

❧

born in Jamaica
moved to England, 1948
critic, teacher
edited *News for Babylon*

Reprinted by permission of Oxford University Press
from Chain of Days © James Berry 1985

The Compton Poetry Fund
Faber and Faber Publishers Ltd
Oxford University Press

Thanks to the ear
that someone may hear

Thanks to seeing
that someone may see

Thanks to feeling
that someone may feel

Thanks to touch
that one may be touched

Thanks to flowering of white moon
and spreading shawl of black night
holding villages and cities together

Over to You

Discover poetry for yourself by collecting examples of everything from short slogans to full length poems. Try to get the widest range possible. This could include children's playground rhymes, advertisements, song lyrics – even graffiti!

Discuss each one, looking particularly for any features which remind you of poetry. It may help you to do this if you ask yourself – in what way does it differ from prose (ordinary writing)? What is the effect of that difference?

Make up some slogans, rhymes and songs of your own based on the ones you have found.

Diversions

One of the most unusual places where you might discover poetry is in graveyards. Most graveyards contain examples of rhyming epitaphs, and occasionally you will find some which are particularly interesting. Read these examples, and then try to discover some for yourself:

Underneath this humble stone,
Sleeps a skull of name unknown,
Deep in Eden's bed Twas found,
Was the luckless owner drowned?
What matter since we all must die,
Whether death be wet or dry?
Kendal, Westmorland

In memory of Benjamin Linton, Blacksmith,
Who died Oct 10 1842 aged 80.

His sledge and hammer lie reclined,
His bellows too have lost their wind,
His fire's extinct, his forge decayed,
His vice all in the dust is laid,
His coal is spent, his iron gone,
His last nail's driven, his work is done.

Blean, Kent

These lines commemorate an organ-blower from Wales:

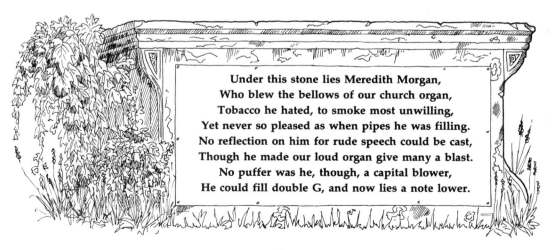

Under this stone lies Meredith Morgan,
Who blew the bellows of our church organ,
Tobacco he hated, to smoke most unwilling,
Yet never so pleased as when pipes he was filling.
No reflection on him for rude speech could be cast,
Though he made our loud organ give many a blast.
No puffer was he, though, a capital blower,
He could fill double G, and now lies a note lower.

2 What is Poetry?

A poem's a poem, man
Keeping in time,
With modern poetry, man
You don't have to rhyme!

No set ways of writing,
Just make up each line,
A poem's a poem, man
You don't have to rhyme.

A poem's a poem,
Just take your time,
Inspiration will come
You don't have to rhyme.

Barbara Zencraft

One of the exciting things about poetry today is its great variety. There are no longer any 'set ways of writing'. Poets can use traditional verse forms if they wish, but they are also free to invent their own. The following selection will give you some idea of the range (some even more surprising 'experiments' with poetry may be found in Chapter 14).

the power of poets

the man on the veranda
outside, giving coppers
to the old tramp and
feeling good isn't me.
I am the veranda.
I could have been
the tramp or even
the coppers. However
I choose to be the
veranda and it is
my poem. Such is
the power of poets.

Roger McGough

MANIC depressant

SOMETIMES I'M HAPPY
sometimes i'm sad;
SoMeTiMeS i'M HsAaPdPY.

Kim Dammers

The inept young person, Miss Muffet,
Had further bad luck with her tuffet;
Some used-tuffet dealers
Decided to steal hers,
So now she must hire one – or rough it.

Dean Walley

OPENING THE CAGE

14 variations on 14 words
I have nothing to say and I am saying it and that is poetry.

John Cage

I have to say poetry and is that nothing and am I saying it
I am and I have poetry to say and is that nothing saying it
I am nothing and I have poetry to say and that is saying it
I that am saying poetry have nothing and it is I and to say
And I say that I am to have poetry and saying it is nothing
I am poetry and nothing and saying it is to say that I have
To have nothing is poetry and I am saying that and I say it
Poetry is saying I have nothing and I am to say that and it
Saying nothing I am poetry and I have to say that and it is
It is and I am and I have poetry saying say that to nothing
It is saying poetry to nothing and I say I have and am that
Poetry is saying I have it and I am nothing and to say that
And that nothing is poetry I am saying and I have to say it
Saying poetry is nothing and to that I say I am and have it

Edwin Morgan

REVOLVER II

Alan Riddell

ON A MIDSUMMER EVE

n
OthI
n
g can
s
urPas
s
the m
y
SteR
y
of
s
tilLnes
s

e e cummings

I idly cut a parsley stalk,
And blew therein towards the moon;
I had not thought what ghosts would walk
With shivering footsteps to my tune.

I went, and knelt, and scooped my hand
as if to drink, into the brook,
And a faint figure seemed to stand
Above me, with the bygone look.

I lipped rough rhymes of chance, not choice,
I thought not what my words might be;
There came into my ear a voice
That turned a tenderer verse for me.

Thomas Hardy

10

Which poem did you most enjoy? What did you like about it?

In your opinion, are any of these examples not really poems at all?

Can you think of a definition of poetry that covers all the examples?

Do not worry if you cannot think of an answer to the last question; you are in good company. Poets and critics throughout the centuries have tried to define poetry but have never quite succeeded in pinning it down, and because new types of poetry are being invented all the time, they probably never will. The following exercises will help you to explore this question for yourself, and if they do not provide you with any neat definitions, they will at least get you thinking and point you in the right direction.

We begin with something familiar – prose. This is the name given to the ordinary kind of writing which we see every day in newspapers, novels and reference books, for example this passage from *Garden and Field Birds*:

Skylark
Alauda arvensis

High in the sky, almost motionless, hovers the skylark, its sweet liquid song filling the air. Between May and July it has two, sometimes three broods. The nest of roots and bits of leaves, lined with hairs and horsehair, is placed on the ground in fields and meadows. The male carefully guards his territory, fiercely fighting to defend it against his rivals. The hen lays three to five eggs which she incubates alone for a period of twelve to fourteen days.

The young are fed with various insects and larvae, centipedes, spiders and small snails by both parents. They leave the nest at the age of nine to eleven days, though as yet incapable of flight, and conceal themselves in clumps of grass. When three weeks old, they are not only able to fly but also to feed themselves. Adult birds also eat the seeds of various weeds which they gather on the ground.

In October–November skylarks form small groups which fly off together to their winter quarters in southern Europe, returning sometimes as early as the end of February when the tang of winter is still in the air and snowfalls not uncommon. Its range of distribution includes the whole of Europe, a large part of Asia and North-west Africa.

Length: 18 cm.
Voice: A clear, liquid "chir-r-up".
Song: Trilling and warbling; sometimes notes learned from other birds.
Size of Egg: 19.4–28.0 × 15.0–19.5 mm.

Notice how the words of this passage run from one side of the page to the other to make the best use of space. The only place where the layout of the words is used to help the meaning is when a line is *indented* to show the start of a paragraph. This emphasises that something new is about to follow.

If we rewrote the passage in a way that made more use of the layout of words, the result would be a kind of poetry. Here are two versions. Read them aloud, and notice how a different layout gives a different emphasis:

High in the sky,
almost motionless,
hovers the skylark,
its sweet liquid song
filling the air.

High

in the sky
hovers

the skylark

its sweet
liquid
song
filling
the air

George Macbeth used this kind of layout in his poem 'Lark' opposite. What does it emphasise?

Try it yourself. Take any piece of prose as a starting point and rewrite it so that the layout emphasises the words and phrases you feel are important.

Another way to change the passage into poetry would be to rewrite it with rhythm and rhyme, like this:

The skylark is seen
hovering high in the sky
singing its sweet liquid song
between May and July.

Try this with your passage – obviously you will have to make quite a few changes, but you must keep to the basic meaning of the original.

These two exercises above focus on some of the techniques that make poetry different from prose: line layout, and rhythm and rhyme. These and many other techniques will be covered in more detail later in this book, but it is important to realise that poetry is more than a collection of techniques: it is a uniquely imaginative way of saying things.

LARK

spi
inn
ng
at
the
pe
ak
of
an
inv
isi
ble
je
t
o
f
w
ate
r,
you
bu
rn
a b
lac
k s
tar
at
th
e h
ear
t
o
f t
he
blu
e a
ppl
e w
e c
all
sk
y,
LARK

George Macbeth

13

The term *verse* is often used to describe writing which uses the techniques of poetry but lacks its imaginative power. The difference can be seen by comparing this poem about a skylark with the passage of 'versified' prose on page 12.

THE ECSTATIC

Lark, skylark, spilling your rubbed and round
Pebbles of sound in air's still lake,
Whose widening circles fill the noon: yet none
Is known so small beside the sun:

Be strong your fervent soaring, your skyward air!
Tremble there, a nerve of song!
Float up there where voice and wing are one,
A singing star, a note of light!

Buoyed, embayed in heaven's noon-wide reaches –
For soon light's tide will turn – oh stay!
Cease not till day streams to the west, then down
That estuary drop down to peace.

C Day Lewis

Try to rewrite 'The Ecstatic' in plain, literal prose, using none of the poet's imaginative comparisons, but leaving out no information. Compare your version with the poem. What has been lost?

Compare 'The Ecstatic' with the prose passage on page 11. What do you learn about the skylark from each? In what way is the use of language different?

So What is Poetry?

Go over this chapter again, discussing the examples on pages 9 and 10 and your responses to the exercises, and jot down some of the ways in which poetry differs from prose.

On page 15 there are some quotations about poetry. Some of the comments are quite surprising. Discuss each one and work out what you think the writer is getting at, then try to work out a definition of your own. You could do this in prose, or you could try a 'list poem' on the subject beginning each line 'A poem is . . .'. Refer back to this page from time to time and reconsider the definitions in the light of your growing knowledge.

I wish our clever young poets would remember my homely definitions of prose and poetry; that is, prose = words in their best order; poetry = the best words in their best order.

Samuel Taylor Coleridge

The poet's eye, in a fine frenzy rolling,
Doth glance from heaven to earth, from earth to heaven;
And, as imagination bodies forth
The forms of things unknown, the poet's pen
Turns them to shapes, and gives to airy nothing
A local habitation and a name.

William Shakespeare

Poetry is simply the most beautiful, impressive and wisely effective mode of saying things, and hence its importance.

Matthew Arnold

Genuine poetry can communicate before it is understood.
T S Eliot

*This definition poetry doth fit,
It is a witty madness, or mad wit.*
Thomas Randolph

A poem is
something that someone is saying
no louder, Pip, than my 'goodnight' –
words with a tune, which outstaying
their speaker travel as far
as that amazing, vibrant light
from a long extinguished star.

Jon Stallworthy

A poet looks at the world as a man looks at a woman.
Wallace Stevens

When power leads man toward arrogance, poetry reminds him of his limitations. When power narrows the area of man's concern, poetry reminds him of the richness and diversity of his existence. When power corrupts, poetry cleanses, for art establishes the basic human truths which must serve as the touchstone of our judgement.

John F Kennedy

15

Diversions

Read this passage, preferably aloud. What is unusual about it?

Obituary

Life's little day is fading fast; upon the mountain's brow, the sinking sun is gleaming red: the shadows lengthen now. The twilight hush comes on apace, and soon the evening star will light us to those chambers dim where dreamless sleepers are; and when the curfew bell has rung that calls us all to rest, and we have left all earthly things at Azrael's request, O may some truthful mourner rise and say of you or me: 'Gee-wiz! I'm sorry that he's dead: he was a honey-bee! Whate'er his job, he did his best: he put on all his steam. In everything he had to do, he was a four-horse team. He thought that man was placed on earth to help his fellow-guys: he never wore a frosty face, and balked at weepy eyes. The hard-luck pilgrim always got a handout at his door; and any friend could help himself to all he had in store. He tried to make his humble home the gayest sort of camp, till Death, the king of bogies, came and slugged him in the lamp. There never was a squarer guy existed in the land; and Death was surely off his base when that galoot was canned.'

Walt Mason

Rewrite it, setting it out as you think it should be set out.

3 *Oral Poetry*

Poetry is the mother tongue of mankind.

Long before most people could read and write, poets made up poems in their heads, remembered them, and recited them on special occasions. People in the audience would remember poems they liked and pass them on to others. Many poems have been passed on for hundreds of years in this way.

This still happens today in a small way – most nursery and playground rhymes are passed on by word of mouth, and you may pick up the words of your favourite pop song simply by listening to the record. But the amazing thing about some of the oral poems of long ago is their great length. Homer's *Odyssey*, for example, is 12,000 lines long, and even when printed makes a very thick book – just imagine trying to remember all that! *Beowulf* is a more recent example from Anglo-Saxon England which was also composed and passed down orally until it was written down in the eighth century. When you read the extract in this chapter, remember that it was originally a kind of performance poetry. The poet would recite its 3,200 lines entirely from memory, accompanying himself on the lyre as he did so. Oral performances very similar to this can still be heard in many parts of the world today, and in Europe and America the idea of performance poetry is making a comeback. An interesting example of this is 'rap'. One rapper from Philadelphia, 'Perry P', can improvise for 50 minutes at a stretch:

> Hiding on the corner
> Of a dark avenue,
> 'Cos you didn't have nothing
> Better to do . . .
> Always have fun,
> Always on the run,
> Can't rap now
> Till I see the sun . . .

You may not be able to manage such a feat, but you can enjoy reading aloud from the following selection of poems. You may even be able to commit one to memory before reciting or performing it.

17

GRENDEL ATTACKS HYGELAC'S HALL

Down off the moorlands' misting fells came
Grendel stalking; God's brand was on him.
The spoiler meant to snatch away
from the high hall some of human race.
he came on under the clouds, clearly saw at last
the gold-hall of men, the mead-drinking place
nailed with gold plates. That was not the first visit
he had paid to the hall of Hrothgar the Dane:
he never before and never after
harder luck not hall-guards found.

Walking to the hall came this warlike creature
condemned to agony. The door gave way,
toughened with iron, at the touch of those hands.
Rage-inflamed, wreckage-bent, he ripped open
the jaws of the hall. Hastening on,
the foe then stepped onto the unstained floor,
angrily advanced: out of his eyes stood
an unlovely light like that of fire.
He saw then in the hall a host of young soldiers,
a company of kinsmen caught away in sleep,
a whole warrior-band. In his heart he laughed then,
horrible monster, his hopes swelling
to a gluttonous meal. He meant to wrench
the life from each body that lay in the place
before night was done. It was not to be;
he was no longer to feast on the flesh of mankind
after that night.
        Narrowly the powerful
kinsman of Hygelac kept watch how the ravager
set to work with his sudden catches;
nor did the monster mean to hang back.
As a first step he set his hands on
a sleeping soldier, savagely tore at him,
gnashed at his bone-joints, bolted huge gobbets,
sucked at his veins, and had soon eaten
all of the dead man, even down to his
hands and feet.

From *Beowulf*, translated by Michael Alexander

From THE MUMMER'S PLAY

[Enter the Presenter]

Presenter I open the door, I enter in;
I hope your favour we shall win.
Stir up the fire and strike a light,
And see my merry boys act to-night.
Whether we stand or whether we fall,
We'll do our best to please you all

[Enter the actors, and stand in a clump]

Presenter Room, room, brave gallants all,
Pray give us room to rhyme;
We're come to show activity,
   This merry Christmas time;
Activity of youth,
Activity of age,
The like was never seen
   Upon a common stage.
And if you don't believe what I say,
Step in St. George – and clear the way.

[Enter St. George]

St. George In come I, Saint George,
   The man of courage bold;
With my broad axe and sword
   I won a crown of gold.
I fought the fiery dragon,
   And drove him to the slaughter,
And by these means I won
   The King of Egypt's daughter.
Show me the man that bids me stand;
I'll cut him down with my courageous hand.

Presenter Step in, Bold Slasher.

[*Enter Bold Slasher*]

Slasher   **In come I, the Turkish Knight,**
    Come from the Turkish land to fight.
I come to fight St. George,
    The man of courage bold;
And if his blood be hot,
    I soon will make it cold.

St. George   **Stand off, stand off, Bold Slasher,**
    And let no more be said,
For if I draw my sword,
I'm sure to break thy head.
Thou speakest very bold,
    To such a man as I;
I'll cut thee into eyelet holes,
    And make thy buttons fly.

Slasher   **My head is made of iron,**
    My body is made of steel,
My arms and legs of beaten brass;
    No man can make me feel.

St. George   **Then draw thy sword and fight,**
    Or draw thy purse and pay;
For satisfaction I must have,
    Before I go away.

Slasher   **No satisfaction shalt thou have,**
    But I will bring thee to thy grave.

St. George   **Battle to battle with thee I call,**
    To see who on this ground shall fall.

Slasher   **Battle to battle with thee I pray,**
    To see who on this ground shall lay.

St. George   **Then guard thy body and mind thy head,**
    Or else my sword shall strike thee dead.

Slasher   **One shall die and the other shall live;**
    This is the challenge that I do give.

[*They fight. Slasher falls*]

Anon

20

SALISBURY PLAIN

As I walked over Salisbury Plain,
Oh, there I met a scamping young blade.
He kissed me and enticed me so
Till along with him I was forced for to go.

We came unto a public house at last,
And there for man and wife we did pass.
He called for ale and wine and strong beer,
Till at length we both to bed did repair.

'Undress yourself, my darling,' says he.
'Undress yourself, and come to bed with me.'
'Oh yes, that I will,' then says she,
'If you'll keep all those flash girls away.'

'Those flash girls you need not fear,
For you'll be safe-guarded, my dear.
I'll maintain you as some lady so gay,
For I'll go a-robbing on the highway.'

Early next morning my love he arose,
And so nimbly he put on his clothes.
Straight to the highway he set sail,
And 'twas there he robbed the coaches of the mail.

Oh, it's now my love in Newgate Jail do lie,
Expecting every moment to die.
The Lord have mercy on his poor soul,
For I think I hear the death-bell for to toll.

Traditional ballad

From THE RAIN-MAKING CEREMONY

RECITATIVE	RESPONSE
We overcome this wind.	We overcome.
We desire the rain to fall, that it be poured in showers quickly.	Be poured.
Ah! thou rain, I adjure thee fall. If thou rainest, it is well.	It is well.
A drizzling confusion.	Confusion.
If it rains and our food ripens, it is well.	It is well
If the children rejoice, it is well.	It is well.
If it rains, it is well. If our women rejoice, it is well.	It is well.
If the young men sing, it is well.	It is well.
A drizzling confusion.	Confusion.
If our grain ripens, it is well.	It is well.
If our women rejoice.	It is well.
If the children rejoice.	It is well.
If the young men sing.	It is well.
If the aged rejoice.	It is well.
An overflowing in the granary.	Overflowing.
May our grain fill the granaries.	May it fill.
A torrent in flow.	A torrent.
If the wind veers to the south, it is well.	It is well.
If the rain veers to the south, it is well.	It is well.

The Lango People, Uganda

TWO CHILDREN'S RHYMES

If you stay to school dinners
Better throw them aside,
A lot of kids didn't
A lot of kids died.
The meat is of iron.
The spuds are of steel,
If that don't get you
Then the afters will.

Latin's a dead language,
As dead as can be.
It killed off the Romans
And now its killing me.

Charlibus sittibus
On the Deskinorum
Deskibus collapsibus
Charlie on the floorum.

WOT A MARF!

Wot a marf' e'd got,
Wot a marf,
When 'e wos a kid,
Goo' Lor' luv'll
'Is pore old muvver
Must 'a' fed 'im wiv a shuvvle.

Wot a gap 'e'd got,
Pore chap,
'E'd never been known to larf,
'Cos if 'e did,
It's a penny to a quid
'E'd 'a' split, 'is fice in 'arf.

Anon

SPRING

Der spring is sprung,
Der grass is riz,
I wonder where dem boidies is?
Der little boids is on der wing,
Ain't dat absoid?
Der little wings is on der boid!

Anon

JOHNNY DOO

Wha lies here,
I, Johnny Doo.
Hee, Johnny, is that you?
Ay, Man, but a'm dead noo.

William Cowper

OOR HAMLET

There was this king sleeping in his gairden a' alane
When his brither in his ear drapped a wee tait o' henbane.
Then he stole his brither's crown and his money and his widow.
But the deid king walked and goat his son and said, 'Heh, listen, kiddo!'
'Ah've been killt and it's your duty to take revenge oan Claudius.
Kill him quick and clean and show the nation whit a fraud he is.'
The boay says, 'Right, Ah'll dae it, but Ah'll huvti play it crafty.
So that naeb'dy will suspect me, Ah'll kid oan that Ah'm a daftie.'

So wi' a' except Horatio (and he trusts him as a friend),
Hamlet – that's the boay – kids oan he's roon the bend,
And because he wisnae ready for obligatory killing
He tried to make the king think he was tuppence aff the shilling!
Took the micky oot Polonius, treatit poor Ophelia vile,
And tellt Rosencrantz and Guildenstern that Denmark was a jile.
Then a troupe o' travelling actors, like 7.84
Arrived to dae a special wan-night gig in Elsinore.

Hamlet, Hamlet! Loved his mammy.
Hamlet, Hamlet! Acting balmy.
Hamlet, Hamlet! Hesitating.
Wonders if the ghost's a cheat and that is why he's waiting.

Then Hamlet wrote a scene for the players to enact,
While Horatio and him would watch to see if Claudius cracked.
The play was ca'd 'The Mousetrap', (No the wan that's running noo)
And sure enough, the king walked oot afore the scene was through.
So Hamlet's goat the proof that Claudius gied his da the dose,
The only problem being noo that Claudius knows he knows.
So while Hamlet tells his ma that her new husband's no a fit wan,
Uncle Claud pits oot a contract wi' the English King as hit-man.

And when Hamlet killed Polonius, the concealed corpus delecti
Was the king's excuse to send him for an English hempen necktie,
Wi' Rosencrantz and Guildenstern to make sure he goat there,
But Hamlet jumped the boat and pit the finger oan that pair.
Meanwhile, Laertes heard his da had been stabbed through the arras;
He came racing back to Elsinore toute-suite, hot-foot fae Paris.
And Ophelia, wi' her da killt by the man she wished to marry –
Efter saying it wi' flooers, she committit hari-kari.

24

Hamlet, Hamlet! Nae messin!
Hamlet, Hamlet! Learnt his lesson.
Hamlet, Hamlet! Yorick's crust
Convinced him that men, good or bad, at last must come to dust.

Then Laertes loast the place and was demanding retribution,
But the king said, 'Keep the heid and Ah'll provide ye a solution.'
And he arranged a sword-fight wi' the interestit perties,
Wi' a bluntit sword for Hamlet and a shairp sword for Laertes.
And to make things double-sure – the auld belt and braces line –
He fixed a poisont sword-tip and a poisont cup o' wine,
And the poisont sword goat Hamlet but Laertes went and muffed it,
'Cause he goat stabbed hissel and he confessed afore he snuffed it.

Then Hamlet's mammy drank the wine and as her face turnt blue,
Hamlet says. 'Ah quite believe the king's a baddy noo.'
'Incestuous, murd'rous, damned Dane,' he said, to be precise,
And made up for hesitating by killing Claudius twice;
'Cause he stabbed him wi' the sword and forced the wine atween his lips
Then he said, 'The rest is silence.' That was Hamlet hud his chips.
They fired a volley ower him that shook the topmost rafter
And Fortinbras, knee-deep in Danes, lived happy ever after.

Hamlet, Hamlet! Aw the gory!
Hamlet, Hamlet! End of story.
Hamlet, Hamlet! Ah'm away!
If you think this is boring, you should read the bloody play!

Adam McNaughtan

THE OXFORD VOICE

When you hear it languishing
and hooing and cooing and sidling through the front
   teeth,
        the oxford voice
           or worse still
      the would-be oxford voice
you don't even laugh any more, you can't.

For every blooming bird is an oxford cuckoo nowadays,
you can't sit on a bus nor in the tube
but it breathes gently and languishingly in the back of
   your neck.

And oh, so seductively superior, so seductively
   self-effacingly
   deprecatingly
    superior. –
We wouldn't insist on it for a moment
    but we are
      we are
    you admit we are
      superior. –

D H Lawrence

A SLUM DWELLER DECLARES

wi wan
fi free
free from misery
wi wan
fi live
like humanbeing
wi nu mean
fi live
pon dump
mongs
dead dawg
an fly
an haffi a fight
johncrow from sky
fi get food fi nyam
wi waan
fi live
like any adda man
yu believe wi com willingly?
yu believe wi waan
wi pickney dem fi grow up
inna place worse dan hag pen?
wi waan
fi live
like humanbeing . . .

Oku Onuora

Rat Rapping

COME ON KEV LET'S GET DOWN TO SOME REAL RAT
RAPPIN YEH HEH
WHAT ARE YOU TALKING ABOUT ROLAND? (RAT RAPPING)
SCRATCHING KEVIN
WHAT RECORDS ROLAND?
NO FLEAS KEVIN FLEAS (RAT RAPPING)
IT'S ALL THE RAGE KEV HEH HEH
FIRST YOU FIND A FLEA PREFERABLY UNDER THE ARMPIT
THEN CHASE IT KEV ROUND YOUR SHOULDERBLADE AND
SCRATCH
(YEAH RAT RAPPING) SCRATCH (YEAH RAT RAPPING)
RIGHT FIRST YOU FIND THE FLEA
YOU'VE GOT IT KEV
I'VE GOT A PROBLEM ROLAND I CAN'T FIND ONE
DON'T BE STUPID KEVIN YOU'RE RIDDLED WITH THEM
AM I ROLAND?
'COURSE YOU ARE DON'T QUESTION ME I'M A SUPERSTAR
PAR EXCELLENCE HEAVY ON STYLE I'M YOUR MAINMAN
SO COME ON KEV MY NUMBER ONE FAN SCRATCH
(YEAH RAT RAPPING) SCRATCH YEAH (RAT RAPPING)
SCRATCH YEAH (RAT RAPPING) SCRATCH YEAH
I DON'T KNOW HOW MANY TIMES I HAVE TO TELL YOU
KEVIN
RATS ARE WONDERFUL RATS ARE MARVELLOUS
THOUSANDS FAINT
AT MY FEET THE WORLD IS MY OYSTER KEV WHY
BECAUSE I'M FULL OF SHOWBIZ GLAMOUR AREN'T I
THE WORLD'S FIRST RODENT SUPERSTAR YEAH
LOTS OF TALK AND LOTS OF ACTION
ROLAND RAT'S THE MAIN ATTRACTION
WITH A PENTHOUSE SUITE SWIMMING POOL
PRETTY YOUNG GUINEA-PIGS PLAYING IT COOL
ROLLS ROYCES YACHTS CAVIAR I TOLD YOU ONCE I'M A
SUPERSTAR
LAH DE DAH LAH DE DEE I'M A MEGASTAR DON'T
QUESTION ME

WANT A CHAUFFEUR WITH A LIMOUSINE (SCRATCH YEAH
RAT RAPPING)
LIVE A LIFE OF LUXURY THAT'S MY DREAM (SCRATCH YEAH)
CARRY CREDIT CARDS DIAMOND RINGS
THESE ARE A FEW OF MY FAVOURITE THINGS
YOU'VE FADED ME OUT KEVIN HOW DARE YOU (SCRATCH)
I JUST THOUGHT YOU WERE GETTING A LITTLE CARRIED
AWAY ROLAND (YEAH)
(SCRATCH YEAH RAT RAPPING SCRATCH RAT RAPPING
SCRATCH YEAH) SCRATCH
I'M SORRY KEVIN I WENT OVER THE TOP A LITTLE I MUST
ADMIT
IT'S JUST THE PRESSURE OF BEING A SUPERSTAR KEV
I KNOW ROLAND YOU ARE WONDERFUL
YEAH WELL WHERE WERE WE OH YEAH SCRATCHING

FINGERS IN THE FUR LET'S FIND THAT FLEA
CHASE IT ON DOWN RIGHT TO THE KNEES
RUN IT AROUND UNTIL YOU CATCH IT
LOCATE THE ITCH AND THEN YOU SCRATCH IT

OH ROLAND I THINK I'M FLEALESS
YEAH WELL OF COURSE YOU WOULD BE WOULDN'T YOU
I'M COVERED IN THEM HANG ON I'VE FOUND ANOTHER ONE
KEV SCRATCH ME KEV (SCRATCH) YEAH (YEAH RAT
RAPPING)
SCRATCH YEAH (RAT RAPPING) SCRATCH YEAH (RAT
RAPPING)
SCRATCH YEAH
YOU'VE GOT THE RIGHT PLACE NOW KEV JUST AT THE
CENTRE OF ME BACK
LOVELY (SCRATCH) YEAH YEAH RAT RAPPING
SCRATCH YEAH RAT RAPPING SCRATCH YEAH RAT
RAPPING
SCRATCH

R Rat

MULE

My Mammy was a wall-eyed goat,
My Old Man was an ass,
And I feed myself off leather boots
And dynamite and grass;
For I'm a mule, a long-eared fool
And I ain't never been to school –
    Mammeee! Ma-ha-mam-hee!
    Heee-haw! Mamaah!
    Ma-ha-mee!

Anon

29

Here are three poems, one apparently written in German and two in French – or are they? Read them aloud and see if you can make sense of them.

MORNING SONG

Horch, horch, die Bell am Backdoor ringt!
Get up! Es iss das Ice.
Ich hoff der Crook von Iceman bringt
A Piece von decent size.
Denn dass gibt shure a Scorcher heut,
Ich fühl alreddy heiss.
Und schlam die Shcreen-thür gut und tight,
Das Haus wird voll mit Flies.
Arise! Arise!
Eh's melten tut, arise!

Kurt M Stein

Lit-elle messe, moffette,
Satan ne te fête,
Et digne somme coeurs et nouez.
À longue qu'aime est-ce pailles d'Eure.
Et ne Satan bise ailleurs
Et ne fredonne messe. Moffette, ah, ouais!

Chacun Gille
Houer ne taupe de hile
Tôt-fait j'appelle au boiteur
Chaque fêle dans un broc, est-ce crosne?
Un Gille qu'aime tant berline à fêtard.

François Charles Fernand d'Antin

Talking Points

How much poetry do you know by heart? Think carefully; you may be surprised how much you know. Do not forget things like rhyming proverbs, rhymes to help you remember facts, Christmas carols and pop songs.

Why is poetry easier to remember than prose?

Can you recognise the different accents and dialects used in some of the poems? What accents and dialects are there in your class?

What is lost when the poems are read silently?

Over to You

Choose a poem which you like, from this book or any other selection, and learn it by heart.

Try to compose a poem entirely in your head, remember it and recite it.

Write a poem in dialect, or one which is specially suited to reading out loud.

Diversions

Here is a real challenge for budding performance poets: can you say these tongue-twisters without tying a knot in your tongue? Say them slowly at first and gradually increase the speed until you reach your limit. Try making up some of your own.

An ex-G.C.E. G.C.S.E. examiner
An ex-G.C.E. G.C.S.E. examiner
An ex-G.C.E. G.C.S.E. examiner

Ned Nott was shot and Sam Shott was not.
So it's better to be Shott than Nott.
Some say Nott was not shot, but Shott swears he shot Nott.
Either the shot Shott shot at Nott was not shot or Nott was shot.
If the shot Shott shot shot Nott, Nott was shot.
But if the shot Shott shot shot Shott himself,
Then Shott would be shot and Nott would not.
However, the shot Shott shot shot not Shott but Nott.
It's not easy to say who was shot and who was not,
But we know who was Shott and who was Nott.

There's no need to light a night light
On a light night like tonight;
For a night light's just a slight light
On a light night like tonight.

4 *Repetition*

Two man a road, Cromanty boy,
Two man a road, fight for you lady!
Two man a road, down town picny,
Two man a road, fight for you lady!
Two man a road, Cromanty win oh!
Two man a road, Cromanty win.

Anon

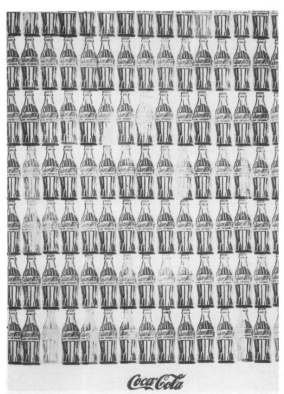

Andy Warhol,
Green Coca-Cola Bottles,
1962

The famous print opposite by Andy Warhol shows how the repetition of a single image can be used to build up a complete picture. This repetition not only creates a pattern, but it helps the artist get his message across. Study the picture for a while and then discuss what you think Andy Warhol is trying to say about Coca-Cola and the society that created it.

Repeated shapes are used in architecture to create form and to emphasise proportions:

Repetition is also used in music. Note how this well-known folk song is built up from a pattern of repeated phrases. Even if you cannot read music, you should be able to see the pattern:

AU CLAIR DE LA LUNE

French folk song

Repeated words and phrases can be used in the same way to create form and to emphasise the writer's message:

EVERY BREATH
YOU TAKE

Every breath you take
Every move you make
Every bond you break
Every step you take
I'll be watching you

Every single day
Every word you say
Every game you play
Every night you stay
I'll be watching you

Oh can't you see
You belong to me
How my poor heart aches, with every step you take

Every move you make
Every vow you break
Every smile you fake
Every claim you stake
I'll be watching you

Since you're gone I've been lost without a trace
I dream at night I can only see your face
I look around but it's you I can't replace
I feel so cold that I long for your embrace
I keep crying baby, baby please

Oh can't you see
You belong to me
How my poor heart aches, with every step you take

Every move you make
Every vow you break
Every smile you fake
Every claim you stake
I'll be watching you

Every move you make
Every step you take
I'll be watching you
I'll be watching you
(Repeat verses to fade)

Sting

34

DIRGE

BODY lies under the ground.
Blow, winds!

Body blows in the sand-dunes.
Blow, winds!

Body drifts in the sea-roads.
Blow, winds!
Blow for the dead.

Body moves much with the farers.
Blow, winds!

Body stares in the snow-lands.
Blow, winds!

Body dooms all the born-ones.
Blow, winds!
Winds blow for the dead.

Gavin Bantock

COLD SONG

The doctor gazed
at the sack of guts passing
and saw
my pretty girl.

The lawyer looked at
a ringless finger
and saw my
pretty girl.

The professor noticed
eyes quick with intelligence
and
saw my pretty girl.

I met my pretty girl
and saw an intelligent
sack of guts with
a ringless finger.

Norman MacCaig

THE STREET

Worms crawling   Worms crawling

    mercedes slides past
    blue shadow

      garbage

swinging   swinging
boozing   boozing

    zephyr slides past
    green shadow

    Wananchi   Wananchi

     scratch
     scratch
     tiny nails
     blocked nostrils

vultures whirr   vultures whirr

    The band splashes
    up the night-club

    rolls-royce
    sleek and cool
    grey shadow

    fireworks
    diwali
    warning light

by shops   by shops

    'closing down sale'
    non-citizen
    gloom   shadow

    mercedes
trinity   mansion   trinity
    shamba

    and the street is clean
    the street is clean

Jared Angira

RASTAFARIAN CHANT

Zion, me wan go home,
Zion, me wan go home,
Oh, Oh,
Zion, me wan go home.

Africa, me wan fe go,
Africa, me wan fe go,
Oh, Oh,
Africa, me wan fe go.

Take me back to Et'iopia lan,
Take me back to Et'iopia lan,
Oh, Oh,
Take me back to Et'iopia lan,

Et'iopia lan me fader's home,
Et'iopia lan me fader's home,
Oh, Oh,
Et'iopia lan me fader's home.

Zion, me wan go home,
Zion, me wan go home,
Oh, Oh,
Zion, me wan go home.

ALWAYS ME

'Can I play?'
'No.'
'Please?'
'No.'
That's the answer, I always get,
Never allowed to play with the older boys,
Or the others.

Always the person to be mocked,
Always the person told off,
Always the person to be pushed around,
Always the person whose rating is down.

Always the cane like a very sharp sword,
Always the cross next to my work,
Always the boredom of work everyday,
I am pounded, pounded,
And the metal's wearing thin!

Ian Jones, aged 15

How has repetition been used to build up the forms of the song 'Every breath you take' and the five poems?

37

IMAGINE

Imagine there's no heaven
It's easy if you try
No hell below us
Above us only sky
Imagine all the people
Living for today . . .

Imagine there's no countries
It isn't hard to do
Nothing to kill or die for
And no religion too
Imagine all the people
Living life in peace . . .

Imagine no possessions
I wonder if you can
No need for greed or hunger
A brotherhood of man
Imagine all the people
Sharing all the world . . .

You may say I'm a dreamer
But I'm not the only one
I hope someday you'll join us
And the world will be as one

John Lennon

IMAGINE

Imagine having all the food you need to keep in your freezer, vacuum sealed in a container this fresh.

Imagine more room in your freezer because each container is the same shape as its contents.

Imagine a container which can be transferred straight from the freezer to the microwave or into boiling water.

That's the idea behind the Pifco Vacuum Bag Sealer.

Special tailor made bags surround your food in seconds with a protective vacuum.

The Pifco Electronic Vacuum Bag Sealer.
The greatest idea since the plastic bag.

Compare the advertisement with John Lennon's song. How do they both use repetition to create a pattern?

Is the advertisement 'Imagine' nearer to prose or poetry? In what ways is it like prose? In what ways is it like poetry? Discuss the way repetition is used – how could it persuade you to buy the product?

38

BREAKFAST

We ate our breakfast lying on our backs
Because the shells were screeching overhead.
I bet a rasher to a loaf of bread
That Hull United would beat Halifax
When Jimmy Stainthorpe played full-back instead
Of Billy Bradford. Ginger raised his head
And cursed, and took the bet, and dropped back dead.
We ate our breakfast lying on our backs
Because the shells were screeching overhead.

Wilfred Gibson

BEWARE OF THE STARS

That star
Will blow your hand off

That star
Will scramble your brains and your nerves

That star
Will frizzle your skin off

That star
Will turn everybody yellow and stinking

That star
Will scorch everything dead fumed to its blueprint

That star
Will make the earth melt

That star . . . and so on.

And they surround us. And far into infinity.
These are the armies of the night.
We are totally surrounded.
There is no escape.
Not one of them is good, or friendly, or corruptible.

One chance remains: KEEP ON DIGGING THAT HOLE

KEEP ON DIGGING AWAY AT THAT HOLE

Ted Hughes

The song '19' was written at a time of renewed interest in the Vietnam War. The film *Rambo* appeared at about the same time.

19

In 1965 Vietnam seemed just like another foreign war.
But it wasn't
It was different in many ways
And so were those who did the fighting
In World War Two the average age of the combat soldier was 26
In Vietnam he was 19, In Vietnam he was 19.
In Vietnam he was 19, In Vietnam he was 19.

19

The heaviest fighting of the past two weeks
Continued today 25 miles north west of Saigon
"I wasn't really sure what was going on"

19, 19, 19, 19

In Vietnam the combat soldier typically served
A twelve-month tour of duty
But was exposed to hostile fire
Almost every day:

19, 19, 19, 19

In Saigon a US military spokesman said today
More than 700 enemy troops were killed last week
In that sensitive border area.
Throughout all of South Vietnam
The enemy lost a total of 2,689 soldiers

All those who remember the war
They won't forget what they've seen
Destruction of men in their prime
Whose average age was 19

D-Destruction, D-Destruction

According to a veterans administration study
Half of the Vietnam combat veterans
Suffer from what psychiatrists call Post Dramatic Stress Disorder
Many vets complain of alienation, rage or guilt
Some succumb to suicidal thoughts
Eight to ten years after coming home
Almost 800,000 men are still fighting the Vietnam war

None of them received a hero's welcome

19, Saigon, Saigon, Saigon, Saigon, Saigon
19, Nineteen, Nineteen, Nineteen, Nineteen
Vietnam, Saigon, Vietnam, Saigon, Vietnam, Saigon,
Vietnam, Saigon
Purple Heart, Saigon, Purple Heart, Saigon
"I wasn't really sure what was going on"
"I wasn't really sure what was going on"

Paul Hardcastle

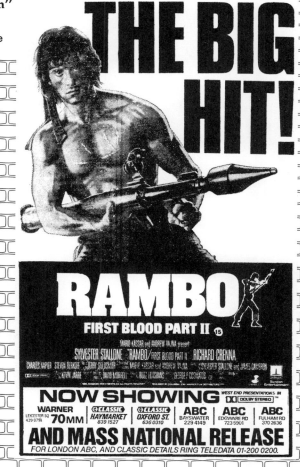

41

TO WHOM IT MAY CONCERN

I was run over by the truth one day.
Ever since the accident I've walked this way
   So stick my legs in plaster
   Tell me lies about Vietnam.

Heard the alarm clock screaming with pain,
Couldn't find myself so I went back to sleep again
   So fill my ears with silver
   Stick my legs in plaster
   Tell me lies about Vietnam.

Every time I shut my eyes all I see is flames.
Made a marble phone book and I carved all the names
   So coat my eyes with butter
   Fill my ears with silver
   Stick my legs in plaster
   Tell me lies about Vietnam.

I smell something burning, hope it's just my brains.
They're only dropping peppermints and daisy-chains
   So stuff my nose with garlic
   Coat my eyes with butter
   Fill my ears with silver
   Stick my legs in plaster
   Tell me lies about Vietnam.

Where were you at the time of the crime?
Down by the Cenotaph drinking slime
   So chain my tongue with whisky
   Stuff my nose with garlic
   Coat my eyes with butter
   Fill my ears with silver
   Stick my legs in plaster
   Tell me lies about Vietnam.

You put your bombers in, you put your conscience out,
You take the human being and you twist it all about
   So scrub my skin with women
   Chain my tongue with whisky
   Stuff my nose with garlic
   Coat my eyes with butter
   Fill my ears with silver
   Stick my legs in plaster
   Tell me lies about Vietnam.

Adrian Mitchell

Compare the song '19' with this poem. What overall impression of the Vietnam War do they give you? Which did you enjoy most? Why?

How has Paul Hardcastle stressed the things he is most concerned about?

Which verses of '19' are like a news report or documentary in style? What are the charcteristics of this style? Why do you think Paul Hardcastle used this style for these verses? How does it add to the effect of the song?

The 'I' in 'To Whom It May Concern' is trying to hide from the truth about the Vietnam War. What is the truth (look at the first two lines of each verse), and how is he trying to hide from it (look at the rest of the verse)? How does repetition emphasise the futility of his attempts to hide from the truth?

Another kind of repetition can be seen in the poem below by Jon Stallworthy, in which the last line of each verse is repeated. This is called a *refrain*. Read the poem and note how the refrain emphasises that the poet in the poem has not experienced the things he is writing about.

A POEM ABOUT POEMS ABOUT VIETNAM

The spotlights had you covered (thunder
in the wings). In the combat zones
and in the Circle, darkness. Under
the muzzles of the microphones
you opened fire, and a phalanx
of loudspeakers shook on the wall;
but all your cartridges were blanks
when you were at the Albert Hall.

Lord George Byron cared for Greece,
Auden and Cornford cared for Spain,
confronted bullets and disease
to make their poems' meaning plain;
but you – by what right did you wear
suffering like a service medal,
numbing the nerve that they laid bare,
when you were at the Albert Hall?

The poets of another time –
Owen with a rifle-butt
between his paper and the slime,
Donne quitting Her pillow to cut
a quill – knew that in love and war
dispatches from the front are all.
We believe them, they were there,
when you were at the Albert Hall.

Poet, they whisper in their sleep
louder from underground than all
the mikes that hung upon your lips
when you were at the Albert Hall.

Jon Stallworthy

43

Over to You

Write about one of the longer poems in this chapter, or about the war poems as a group. Use or adapt this suggested plan:

- Write a short introduction in which you say simply and clearly what the poem is about.

- Write about the way repetition has been used.

- Conclude with your personal response to the poem – for example, what did you like/dislike about it? Which parts did you find particularly interesting and effective? What thoughts and feelings did it leave you with?

Write your own poems or songs using the ideas in ths chapter for inspiration. Experiment with different kinds of repetition.

Diversions

Read the following pop song which has been written by a budding songwriter. Give your opinion of it, pointing out its good and bad qualities, and giving suggestions for improvement. Compare your comments with those given on page 165.

> The sun is shining on my head
> and I am lying on my couch
> Someone hits me on the nose
> Ouch I cry, that was sore
>
> Oh yeah, Oh yeah, Oh yeah
> Oh yeah, Oh yeah, Oh yeah
> Oh yeah, Oh yeah, Oh yeah
> Oh yeah, Oh yeah, Oh yeah
>
> Mash, Mashie Mask, Mask
> Maskar, Maskinonge, Masochism
> Mason, Mason-Dixon, Masonry
> Masorah, Masorete, Masque
>
> Oh yeah, Oh yeah, Oh yeah (×146)
>
> My pink toothbrush melts in the purple sun
> and seven chocolate horsemen get a
> plastic parking ticket
>
> Oh yeah, Oh yeah, Oh yeah . . .
> (fade)

5 Rhyme

Here lies John Payne
Who was killed by a train.
(He was really drowned in a flood
But that wouldn't rhyme, but 'train' would).

Anon

Rhyme is the musical effect created when two words end with the same sound. It is the best known poetic technique – so well known in fact, that many people think that a poem without rhyme is not a poem at all! This attitude is responsible for many clumsily written verses that seem to have been tortured into rhyme at all costs – even when it muddles the meaning!

However, when rhyme is used well, it can give emphasis in the right places, as well as adding the beauty of its musical effect:

ON A SUNDIAL

I am a sundial, and I make a botch
Of what is done far better by a watch.

Anon

In this epigram the key words 'botch' and 'watch' are emphasised, and the two lines are neatly tied together by the rhyme, making a complete and satisfying whole.

Rhyme is also used to create form. The epigram 'On a Sundial' is one of the simplest examples: the *couplet*. Another simple form is the *quatrain* with alternate rhymes:

I travelled among unknown men,
In lands beyond the sea;
Nor, England! did I know till then
What love I bore to thee.

William Wordsworth

45

How has rhyme been used to emphasise the message of the advertisements below and opposite? Which key words are emphasised?

Find other rhyming advertisements and study them in the same way.

When Christmas is over, the last cracker cracked,

The turkey's a carcass and don't you feel whacked,

Pine needles are falling, the kids' toys are broken,

Look on the bright side you still have a Book Token.

You have a treat in store for a cold day in January.

When everyone else is cutting back, you can walk into pretty well any bookshop and experience the delicious freedom of buying books with someone else's money.

You'll find your eyes lingering over those expensive art books and even the ultimate luxury, hardback novels.

Enjoy it, courtesy of Book Tokens Ltd and your generous donor.

Remember, after Christmas only comes but once a year.

Book Tokens

Many other rhyme schemes can be found in the poems and advertisements in this chapter, but the important thing is to notice the way in which rhyme is *used* – what does it emphasise? How does it add to the music of the poem? How does it create form?

AN AUGUST MIDNIGHT

A shaded lamp and a waving blind,
And the beat of a clock from a distant floor:
On this scene enter – winged, horned, and spined –
A longlegs, a moth, and a dumbledore;
While 'mid my page there idly stands
A sleepy fly, that rubs its hands . . .

Thus meet we five, in this still place,
At this point of time, at this point in space.
My guests besmear my new-penned line,
Or bang at the lamp and fall supine.
'God's humblest, they!' I muse. Yet why?
They know Earth-secrets that know not I.

                                        Thomas Hardy

DEATH OF A FLY

Raising my pen to put a point
On the page – a dot on an 'i'
An unsteadily veering fly
Settles. Then, as if carving a joint
It carefully sharpens its legs,
Sitting up the way a dog begs.
My pen moves – and it's off again
Colliding clumsily with my pen.
I notice a wing shed like a petal
Its soft tissue torn on the metal.
It has come here to die
In the place where I dotted the 'i'
And my dot, streaked now with blood
Turns the colour of mud.

                                        Alan Ross, aged 14

Alan Ross' poem was inspired by reading 'An August Midnight' by Thomas Hardy. Compare the two: which parts of Hardy's poem did Alan respond to? Why do you think Alan chose a different rhyme scheme?

Find a rhyming poem which you particularly like and use it as the basis of a poem of your own.

COMPOSED UPON WESTMINSTER BRIDGE

Earth has not anything to show more fair:
Dull would he be of soul who could pass by
A sight so touching in its majesty:
This City now doth, like a garment, wear
The beauty of the morning; silent, bare,
Ships, towers, domes, theatres, and temples lie
Open unto the fields, and to the sky;
All bright and glittering in the smokeless air.
Never did sun more beautifully steep
In his first splendour, valley, rock, or hill;
Ne'er saw I, never felt, a calm so deep!
The river glideth at his own sweet will:
Dear God! the very houses seem asleep;
And all that mighty heart is lying still!

William Wordsworth

Old Westminster Bridge in 1754

49

LONDON

I wander thro' each charter'd street,
Near where the charter'd Thames does flow,
And mark in every face I meet
Marks of weakness, marks of woe.

In every cry of every Man,
In every Infant's cry of fear,
In every voice, in every ban,
The mind-forg'd manacles I hear.

How the chimney-sweeper's cry
Every black'ning church appalls;
And the hapless soldier's sigh
Runs in blood down palace walls.

But most thro' midnight streets I hear
How the youthful harlot's curse
Blasts the new-born infant's tear,
And blights with plagues the marriage hearse.

William Blake

A LONDON SPRING

The quiet pavements of the morning gleam
With dew, the roofs are razor-bright
In sun, and from a memory of night
The blue day rises like a misty dream.

At noon our shadow walks beside us like a dog.
Behind the radiant windows of the afternoon
Our secret thoughts remember a forgotten tune
Played in a peaceful street, in autumn fog.

Now in the early evening light
Trees drift, as we walk, like pale clouds
Of green through the indifferent crowds;
And lamps like crystal birds sing in the leaves of night.

James Kirkup

Compare the different views of London in 'Composed upon Westminster Bridge',
'London' and 'A London Spring'. Which key words are emphasised by rhyme?

Notice how the pattern of rhymes creates a verse form. Choose one of the rhyme-
schemes for a poem of your own. Note that more information about rhyme and rhyme-
schemes may be found in the Glossary on page 167.

Rhyme is often used to express humour, the rhyme emphasising the punchline of the
joke. Multi-syllable rhymes such as 'relations/conversations' are particularly effective –
so much so that they have to be used with care in serious poetry to avoid an
unintentional humorous effect.

THE PRACTICAL JOKER

Oh, what a fund of joy jocund lies hid in harmless hoaxes!
    What keen enjoyment springs
    From cheap and simple things!
What deep delight from sources trite inventive humour coaxes,
    That pain and trouble brew
    For every one but you!
Gunpowder placed inside its waist improves a mild Havana,
    Its unexpected flash
    Burns eyebrows and moustache.
When people dine no kind of wine beats ipecacuanha,
    But common sense suggests
    You keep it for your guests –
Then naught annoys the organ boys like throwing red hot coppers.
    And much amusement bides
    In common butter slides;
And stringy snares across the stairs cause unexpected croppers.
    Coal scuttles, recollect,
    Produce the same effect.
      A man possessed
        Of common sense
      Need not invest
        At great expense –
      It does not call
        For pocket deep,
      These jokes are all
        Extremely cheap.
If you commence with eighteenpence – it's all you'll have to pay;
You may command a pleasant and a most instructive day.

A good spring gun breeds endless fun, and makes men jump like
    rockets –
        And turnip heads on posts
        Make very decent ghosts.
Then hornets sting like anything, when placed in waistcoat
    pockets –
        Burnt cork and walnut juice
        Are not without their use.
No fun compares with easy chairs whose seats are stuffed with
    needles –
        Live shrimps their patience tax
        When put down people's backs.
Surprising, too, what one can do with a pint of fat black beetles –
        And treacle on a chair
        Will make a Quaker swear!
          Then sharp tin tacks
            And pocket squirts –
        And cobbler's wax
            For ladies' skirts –
        And slimy slugs
            On bedroom floors –
        And water jugs
            On open doors –
Prepared with these cheap properties, amusing tricks to play
Upon a friend a man may spend a most delightful day.

Sir W S Gilbert

Read the poem 'Attack on the Ad-Man' opposite and then consider the following
questions.

What techniques or tricks does the Ad-man use to make us buy?

Which words are emphasised by rhyme? Why are these words important?

Can you find any of these techniques in the advertisements in this book or in any
magazines or newspapers?

Poets and advertisers both use words skilfully to get a message across.

● What is the advertiser's aim?

● What is the poet's aim?

● Discuss the difference in these aims.

Why does the Ad-Man's use of words leave them 'shabby, worn, diminished, mean'
(verse 3)? How would a poet's use of words leave them?

ATTACK ON THE AD-MAN

This trumpeter of nothingness, employed
To keep our reason dull and null and void,
This man of wind and froth and flux will sell
The wares of any who reward him well.
Praising whatever he is paid to praise,
He hunts for ever-newer, smarter ways
To make the gilt seem gold; the shoddy, silk;
To cheat us legally; to bluff and bilk
By methods which no jury can prevent
Because the law's not broken, only bent.

This mind for hire, this mental prostitute
Can tell the half-lie hardest to refute;
Knows how to hide an inconvenient fact
And when to leave a doubtful claim unbacked;
Manipulates the truth but not too much,
And, if his patter needs the Human Touch,
Skilfully artless, artfully naïve,
Wears his convenient heart upon his sleeve.

He uses words that once were strong and fine,
Primal as sun and moon and bread and wine,
True, honourable, honoured, clear and clean,
And leaves them shabby, worn, diminished, mean.
He takes ideas and trains them to engage
In the long little wars big combines wage.
He keeps his logic loose, his feelings flimsy;
Turns eloquence to cant and wit to whimsy;
Trims language till it fits his client's pattern
And style's a glossy tart or limping slattern.

He studies our defences, find the cracks
And, where the wall is weak or worn, attacks.
He finds the fear that's deep, the wound that's tender,
And, mastered, outmanoeuvred, we surrender.
We who have tried to choose accept his choice
And tired succumb to his untiring voice.
The dripping tap makes even granite soften.
We trust the brand-name we have heard so often
And join the queue of sheep that flock to buy;
We fools who know our folly, you and I.

A S J Tessimond

53

GIRL REPORTER

Fact is her fiction. Sitting in a bar
Raincoat still on, crossed nylon legs revealing
Less than we think, a male in tow and smiling –
Her narrowed eyes flick past to register
Whether I am a story in the offing.

Life is material for her creation.
The doll by the up-turned scooter – that is real,
Its head, see, stains the kerb. She runs to call
The news desk first, then after the police-station,
Already mapping the story of the trial.

Errors of fact are part of her prose style.
With every slashing cross-head some truth dies.
In love? She knows. You hate her? She knows.
     You'll
Cure cancer? Reach the moon? Her face may smile –
You're placed by those all-knowing know-all eyes.

What chance has truth against such showy error?
We're butterflies pinned down by this young lady,
Facts of our lives are melted down for cliché.
Even as I write her gaze observes my tremor –
Her lethal pencil always at the ready.

Philip Hobsbaum

Compare the use of rhyme in 'Girl Reporter' and 'Gutter Press'. In which poem has rhyme been used with greater freedom?

Do you think the headlines in 'Gutter Press' are real, or made up? How can you tell?

What is the difference between the attitude of the Cameraman and that attitude of the News Editor? How is rhyme used to emphasise the News Editor's attitude? Whose attitude do you think is morally right, and whose do you think is likely to sell most newspapers?

J.P. Goes
To Jug

Peer Confesses

GUTTER PRESS

**Baronet
Bottled**

Holiday of
Horror

Sex in Yarmouth

Tanks in
Terror Hunt

Bishop
Undresses

**Show Girl
Beaten**

Mate Drugs
Purser

I Quit

Jail Rampage Probe

Eminent Hostess Shoots
Her Guests

**Terror
At
Beauty
Spot**

**Wrecks off
Barmouth**

*Strikers
Rampage*

Judge
Gets
Frisky

Scandal

News editor: Peer Confesses,
Bishop Undresses,
Torso Wrapped in Rug,
Girl Guide Throttled,
Baronet Bottled,
J.P. Goes to Jug.

But yesterday's story's
Old and hoary.
Never mind who got hurt.
No use grieving,
Let's get weaving.
What's the latest dirt?

Diplomat Spotted,
Scout Garrotted,
Thigh Discovered in Bog,
Wrecks Off Barmouth,
Sex in Yarmouth
Woman In Love With Dog,
Eminent Hostess Shoots Her Guests,
Harrogate Lovebird Builds Two Nests.

Cameraman: *Builds two nests?*
Shall I get a picture of the lovebird singing?
Shall I get a picture of her pretty little eggs?
Shall I get a picture of her babies?

News Editor: No!
Go and get a picture of her legs.

Beast Slays Beauty,
Priest Flays Cutie,
Cupboard Shows Tell-Tale Stain,
Mate Drugs Purser,
Dean Hugs Bursar,
Mayor Binds Wife With Chain,
Elderly Monkey Marries For Money,
Jilted Junky Says 'I Want My Honey'.

55

Motorway madness Disaster

Grim Day

Jeers Censorship

Concern Suicide Strike

Paranoia Shame

Pit Flood Guilt

Terror

Cameraman: *'Want my honey?'*
Shall I get a picture of the pollen flying?
Shall I get a picture of the golden dust?
Shall I get a picture of a queen bee?

News Editor: No!
Go and get a picture of her bust.

Judge Gets Frisky,
Nun Drinks Whisky,
Baby Found Burnt in Cot,
Show Girl Beaten,
Duke Leaves Eton –

Cameraman: *Newspaper Man Gets Shot!*
May all things clean
And fresh and green
Have mercy upon your soul,
Consider yourself paid
By the hole my bullet made –

News Editor: (*dying*) Come and get a picture of the hole.

Paul Dehn

Some of the most difficult rhyming forms have been borrowed from the French – a language with many more rhyming words than English. The *ballade*, the *villanelle* and the *rondeau* are so difficult in English that they are almost impossible (try one yourself, and see – you will find an explanation of these forms in the Glossary, page 167). The two rondeaux below make an interesting comparison. The subject of William Jay Smith's rondeau is the very difficulty of writing one, and this gives him an excellent excuse for any awkward moments, such as bringing in 'Sono Osato' just to keep to the rhyme scheme. What other awkward moments can you find? On the other hand, Thomas Hardy manages the demanding rhyme scheme with such ease that you would not realise there was anything especially difficult about the form he has chosen:

RONDEAU

Lord, I'm done for: now Margot
Insists I write her a rondeau.
   Just to think of it gives me pain:
   Eight 'o' lines and five in 'ain' –
A slow boat to China is not so slow.

With five lines down, and eight to go,
I summon Sono Osato,
   Adding, with an eye for gain,
      Lord, I'm done.

If from my brain five others flow
My poem will in beauty grow:
   Comes eleven, that is plain,
   And twelve to follow in its train,
And so thirteen rounds out the show –
      Lord, I'm done!

William Jay Smith

THE ROMAN ROAD

The Roman Road runs straight and bare
As the pale parting-line in hair
   Across the heath. And thoughtful men
   Contrast its days of Now and Then,
And delve, and measure, and compare;

Visioning on the vacant air
Helmed legionaries, who proudly rear
   The Eagle, as they pace again
      The Roman Road.

But no tall brass-helmed legionnaire
Haunts it for me. Uprises there
   A mother's form upon my ken,
   Guiding my infant steps, as when
We walked that ancient thoroughfare,
      The Roman Road.

Thomas Hardy

Over to you

Write in detail about one of the poems or groups of poems in this chapter. Begin by explaining what the poet is saying and show how rhyme is used to emphasise this message. Comment on any other interesting features, and conclude by writing about your personal reaction to the poem and the ideas in it.

Write your own 'Attack on the Ad-man' in poetry or any other form.

Write a poem based on newspaper headlines. Use the ones on pages 55 and 56 for inspiration.

Browse through some poetry anthologies looking for different rhyme schemes. Look particularly for the way rhyme is used to help the poet communicate more effectively. Experiment with different rhyme schemes.

Diversions

Use the skills you have acquired so far to help you solve this puzzle. On pages 58 and 59 are two poems. One is by an unknown amateur poet, the other is by a modern poet with several publications. Can you tell which is which? The answer is on page 165.

- Look at the use of rhyme. Is it skilful and effective, or is it sometimes clumsy?

- Listen to the rhythm of each poem. Does it flow naturally, or are there awkward halts and jerks?

- Which poem has the most interesting and well-expressed subject?

- Think about these points, make up your mind which is which, and then when the rest of the class is ready, be prepared to discuss your answer and give reasons for it.

NOTES FOR A MOVIE SCRIPT

Fade in the sound of summer music,
Picture a hand plunging through her hair,
Next his socked feet and her scuffed dance slippers
Close, as they kiss on the rug-stripped stair.

Catch now the taxi from the station,
Capture her shoulders' sudden sag;
Switch to him silent in the barracks
While the room roars at the corporal's gag.

Let the drums dwindle in the distance,
Pile the green sea above the land;
While she prepares a single breakfast,
Reading the V-Mail in her hand.

Ride a cold moonbeam to the pillbox,
Sidle the camera to his feet
Sprawled just outside in the gummy grasses,
Swollen like nightmare and not neat.

Now doorbell nudges the lazy morning:
She stills the sweeper for a while,
Twitches her dress, swings the screendoor open,
Cut – with no music – on her smile.

Carl Holman

STAR QUALITY

I wish I could star in a movie –
Trouble is, I'm no smoothie,
I'm not as good-looking as Robert Redford,
And my car's not a Porsche, it's a rust-red Ford!

I'm not as mean
Or as cool as James Dean,
Sylvester Stallone's muscles are bigger,
And my girlfriend hasn't got Bo Derek's good looks.

I'm no good at romance,
I can't dance or sing,
I've got no tact or charm –
I can't even act!

If I could just be in a movie
The tiniest bit-part would do me:
If I was allowed
Just to be in a large group of people,
I'd earn more applause
Than the shark in 'Jaws'!
(From my neighbours at any rate!)

But I have to admit
There's not much chance of that,
So I've bought a video camera,
And though my girlfriend's short on glamour, her
Face is all I've got!
(I tried to get Bridgit Bardot,
But she said no!)
So I hope my girlfriend's figure
And Frankenstein-like features do not mar
The film I'm going to make – 'cause I'm the star!

Arthur Metcalf

What qualities make a good poem, i.e. why is one better than the other?

Rewrite the poem by the amateur poet and see if you can improve it.

6 Pen Rhythms

Well listen everybody let me tell you 'bout rock 'n' roll
Oh feel that rhythm and its really gonna thrill your soul

ELO

I would define, in brief, the Poetry of words as the
Rhythmical Creation of Beauty.

Edgar Allen Poe

When people listen to pop music they often tap their feet, twitch their bodies or nod their heads. They are enjoying the *rhythm* or 'beat' of the music. Words also have rhythm, and though a poem is not likely to set you tapping your feet, its rhythm can still be heard and enjoyed.

A rhythm is heard because some syllables (see the Glossary page 167) are spoken with heavier stress than others. Read this limerick aloud and see if you can hear the stressed syllables and the rhythm they create:

> There was a young man of Montrose
> Who had pockets in none of his clothes.
> When asked by his lass
> Where he carried his brass
> He said 'Darling, I pay through the nose.'

Arnold Bennett

When stressed syllables are arranged in a pattern, four per line for example, the result is called *metre*. Metre is a regular pulse running through a poem which highlights any variations in rhythm, and it is the rhythm that is the important thing as it can be used to create many effects. A good example of this is the passage below from a poem by Alexander Pope. The metre is a regular five stresses per line (except the last, which has six) and this highlights the changes of rhythm, from slow and laboured (Ajax throwing a rock) to quick and light (Camilla flying):

The sound must seem an echo to the sense:
Soft is the strain when zephyr gently blows,
And the smooth stream in smoother numbers flows;
But when loud surges lash the sounding shore,
The hoarse, rough verse should like the torrent roar:
When Ajax strives some rock's vast weight to throw,
The line too labours, and the words move slow;
Not so, when swift Camilla scours the plain,
Flies o'er the unbending corn, and skims along the main.

A detailed study of metre and rhythm would be quite complicated. If you wish to find out more, look up the terms in the Glossary, page 167. Fortunately, it is not necessary to understand all the technicalities to appreciate the effects they can create. If you read the following poems and songs aloud, you should hear the effects of metre and rhythm quite clearly.

THE PRAISE OF DANCING

'Dancing, bright lady, then began to be,
   When the first seeds whereof the world did spring,
The fire, air, earth, and water, did agree
   By Love's persuasion, nature's mighty king,
   To leave their first discorded combating,
      And in a dance such measure to observe,
      As all the world their motion should preserve.

'Since when they still are carried in a round,
   And changing come one in another's place;
Yet do they neither mingle nor confound,
   But every one doth keep the bounded space
   Wherein the dance doth bid it turn or trace.
      This wondrous miracle did Love devise,
      For dancing is love's proper exercise.'

Sir John Davies

DANCING IN
THE STREET

Ok
Tokyo
South America
Australia
France
Germany
UK
Africa

Calling out around the world
Are you ready for a brand new beat
Summer's here and the time is right
For dancing in the street (dancing in the street)
They're dancin' in Chicago (dancing in the street)
Down in New Orleans (dancing in the street)
In New York City (dancing in the street)
All we need is music (sweet sweet) sweet music (sweet sweet music)
There'll be music everywhere (everywhere)
There'll be swinging swaying and records playing
Dancing in the street oh

62

It doesn't matter what you wear
Just as long as you are there
So come on every guy grab a girl
Everywhere around the world
There'll be dancing dancing in the street (dancing in the street)
It's an invitation across the nation
A chance for folks to meet
There'll be laughing and singing and music swinging
Dancing in the street
Philadelphia P.A. (dancing in the street)
Baltimore and D.C. now (dancing in the street)
Don't forget the Motor City (dancing in the street)
On the streets of Brazil (dancing in the street)
Back in the USSR (dancing in the street)
Don't matter where you are (dancing in the street)
All we need is music (sweet sweet) sweet music
(Sweet sweet music)
There'll be music everywhere (everywhere)
There'll be swinging swaying and records playing
Dancing in the street oh
It doesn't matter what you wear
Just as long as you are there
So come on every guy grab a girl
Everywhere around the world

There'll be dancing they're dancing in the street
(Dancing in the street)
Way down in L.A.
Ev'ry day they're dancing in the street (dancing in the street)
Across in China to me and you
Dancing in the street (dancing in the street)
Don't you know that we're dancing

ad lib to fade

William Stevenson, Marvin Gaye and Ivy Hunter

REASONS FOR ATTENDANCE

The trumpet's voice, loud and authoritative,
Draws me a moment to the lighted glass
To watch the dancers – all under twenty-five –
Shifting intently, face to flushed face,
Solemnly on the beat of happiness.

– Or so I fancy, sensing the smoke and sweat,
The wonderful feel of girls. Why be out here?
But then, why be in there? Sex, yes, but what
Is sex? Surely, to think the lion's share
Of happiness is found by couples – sheer

Inaccuracy, as far as I'm concerned.
What calls me is that lifted, rough-tongued bell
(Art, if you like) whose individual sound
Insists I too am individual
It speaks; I hear; others may hear as well,

But not for me, nor I for them; and so
With happiness. Therefore I stay outside,
Believing this; and they maul to and fro,
Believing that; and both are satisfied,
If no one has misjudged himself. Or lied.

Philip Larkin

REGGAE SOUNDS

Shock-black bubble-doun-beat bouncing
rock-wise tumble-doun soun music:
foot-drop find drum blood story;
bass history is a moving
        is a hurting black story.

Thunder from a bass drum sounding,
lightening from a trumpet and a organ;
bass and rhythm and trumpet double-up,
team up with drums for a deep doun searching.

Rhythm of a tropical electrical storm
(cooled doun to the pace of the struggle)
flame-rhythm of historically yearning,
flame-rhythm of the time of turning,
measuring the time for bombs and for burning.

slow drop. make stop. move forward.
dig doun to the root of the pain;
shape it into violence for the people,
they will know what to do they will do it.

Shock-black bubble-doun-beat bouncing
rock-wise tumble-doun soun music:
foot-drop find drum blood story;
bass history is a moving
        is a hurting black story.

L K Johnson

How does the rhythm of 'Reggae Sounds' echo the meaning of the poem?

How is the sound of certain letters used to suggest a rhythmic beat, or a bass drum?

ROCKING
GRAN BLUES

Who says I'm too old for the disco?
While the music still touches me soul,
While I dance in bare feet and move with the beat
And me feet turn as black as the coal.
Oh just say the word, young Adonis!
I'll reggae with you till it's day,
Just lend me a fag and pass us me bag
For me Pan Stick has all run away.

Oh yes, I know you've seen nothing like it!
My dancing is lissom and free!
Take a look round the place, each wondering face,
Everyone's looking at me!
Oh take it away, lay it on me!
We'll tear up the floor through the night,
We'll be rocking and reeling while the ball on the ceiling
Festoons us in speckles of light.

I've scraped all me hair in a beehive,
I've stapled it up at the back,
Though once it was pepper and salt, dear,
Now it is ebony black.
Tell the deejay to turn up the volume!
Turn it up with no fear of reproof!
So we hear the pound and the pulsating sound
And the woodworm all fall out the roof.

For there's nothing like music to get you,
Oh the shivers it sends down your back,
And if you're approaching the bar, dear,
I'll have a nice rum and black.
And get me a packet of crisps, dear,
Bacon or onion will do
And then *mon amour* we'll give it what for
And dance till our faces turn blue.

And then in my clapped out Ford Consul,
Parked by a rippling stream,
I'll flash you a smile, find the spot on the dial
And cover the windows with steam.
It's the wonderful weekend for working,
So until Monday when we clock on
Take my hand in the dark, out in the car park
It's Saturday evening: rock on.

Pam Ayres

66

How does the rhythm add to the humour of 'Rocking Gran Blues'? What well-known humorous verse form does the rhythm suggest?

ELVIS PRESLEY

Two minutes long it pitches through some bar:
Unreeling from a corner box, the sigh
Of this one, in his gangling finery
And crawling sideburns, wielding a guitar.

The limitations where he found success
Are ground on which he, panting, stretches out
In turn, promiscuously, by every note.
Our idiosyncrasy and likeness.

We keep ourselves in touch with a mere dime:
Distorting hackneyed words in hackneyed songs
He turns revolt into a style, prolongs
The impulse to a habit of the time.

Whether he poses or is real, no cat
Bothers to say: the pose held is a stance,
Which, generation of the very chance
It wars on, may be posture for combat.

Thom Gunn

The rhythm of the poem 'Elvis Presley' is based on a simple metrical pattern, and it is therefore a good place to start a closer study of metre. Copy out the first verse and make a study of the metre of the poem as explained in the Glossary on page 167.

The poem by Thom Gunn inspired Lisa Bishop to write her own tribute to Elvis. Why not write a poem about your favourite pop singer?

ELVIS

He was the greatest rocker ever
But now he has gone forever.
He was called the King of rock
And his death was such a shock.
His hits were always number one
And will remind us of him now he's gone.
He made the girls shout and scream
But Priscilla was the only one for him.
Tragedy struck – the death of his mother
And Priscilla leaving him for another,
His health declined when he came to depend
On drugs and alcohol which caused his tragic end.
Now he has gone forever
But his songs will be forgotten never.

Lisa Bishop, aged 16

Talking Points

What other areas of human activity and art involve rhythm? Why do we have such a deep appreciation of rhythm? What is rhythmic in the human body and in nature?

Over to You

Go back over some of the poems you have studied in earlier chapters and look at their rhythm. You could ask yourself these questions about each poem:

- Is the rhythm free, like prose, or is there some kind of 'beat' to it?

- Can you hear a regular metre in the rhythm of the poem?

- Has the poet used rhythm to create any effects or emphasise the meaning of the poem?

Find examples of other poems written in regular metre, or where rhythm has been used for special effect. An anthology of traditional verse would be a good place to look. Limericks should also provide a happy hunting ground. Hymn books, though somewhat less amusing than limericks, are particularly interesting, because they usually contain an index classifying tunes according to metre.

Diversions

Complete this poem giving particular attention to rhyme and rhythm. Read it through (what there is of it!) to get the feel of the rhythm and the simple rhyme scheme and then copy it out filling in the gaps as you go. Note that there is no one 'correct' version of this poem. Any version that makes sense, and which fits the pattern of rhythm and rhyme, is correct. Why not add more verses too?

My mum tells me not to wear make-up
But I will if I want to, so there!
How can a young woman look pretty
When her features are practically bare!

I'd feel _____ without it
Although I am only fourteen

_____

_____ to be seen.

Foundation cream, _____ and_____
Eye-liner, lipstick and _____
Nail-varnish _____

_____

That's only the start, next there's _____

_____

_____

_____

And now to get dressed. Where's my _____
My _____ and my high-heeled shoes?
My _____

_____

That's better! I'm fit for a disco,
Though _____ still thinks I'm a fool,
Just a final touch-up with that _____ –
That's it – now I'm ready for _____!

7 Free Verse

There was a young poet of Trinity
Who, although he could trill like a linnet, he
   Could never complete
   Any poems with feet,
Saying, 'Idiots,
   Can't you see
   That what I'm writing
     happens
     to be
     Free
Verse?'

Anon

Writing rhymed metrical verse can be very frustrating. You may have a good idea or a striking image, but be unable to find a word that rhymes, or has the right number of syllables. One solution to this problem is to write *free verse*, which has no regular rhyme or metre. Free verse was introduced by the American poet Walt Whitman about a hundred years ago, though at first most people were horrified that he dared to call it poetry. However, it has slowly gained in popularity, and is now the form used by most modern poets.

Free verse has many advantages over rhymed metrical verse. For example, it gives poets the freedom to set out words and lines in any way they like to create special effects, to create patterns with words, and to create their own flexible rhythms.

Look out for these features as you read the following poems:

IF LIFE'S A LOUSY PICTURE, WHY NOT LEAVE BEFORE THE END

Don't worry
One night we'll find that deserted kinema
The torches extinguished
The cornish ripples locked away in the safe
The tornoff tickets chucked
In the tornoff shotbin
the projectionist gone home to his nightmare

Don't worry
that film will still be running
(the one about the sunset)
& we'll find two horses
tethered in the front stalls
& we'll mount
& we'll ride off
                    into
                        our
                            happy
                                ending

Roger McGough

THE SWIMMING POOL

Chlorine overpowers everything
Wet floors, drained benches,
Echoes of resounding splashes burnt through the doors,
Jaunty water ripples in dazzling sunlight.
Shrieks and shouts; everybody's
In a world of their own.
Water! A new dimension of acrobatics,
Movement, constant motion.
Take a sharp header in! Hear the explosion.
Swim through tickling bubbles!
Break the surface in triumph!
Shake back wet hair, streaming over misty eyes.
Showered in spray from mysterious antics.
Water! Space men bounce on the bottom,
Shadows rush up, suddenly springing into
Sharp focus. Turn away in a flurry of bubbles.
Bodies everywhere, thin statures, flabby loose skins,
Bedraggled hair. Frilly caps. Fancy suits.
All part of the swimming pool!

Alison Rostron, aged 14

71

THE WAY YOU DANCE IS THE WAY I LIVE

dancehall   the
  people all   doing

the
  same   each
    things

one   pivoting the

same   graceless
    arc
     of
      aching empty
        hope
         less
         hope

strange but they never meet
  the way they dance
 is   the way i
   live

Martin Ward

SNOOKER PLAYER

He is a general.
He arranges ivory sounds.

He begins by breaking
The symmetry of delta.

He is a general
He has enemies:
They are colours.

He aims to finish
With an empty field.

Shhh!
He is a general.
Words are a distraction.

The object of his game
Is complete silence.

Richard Freeman

Study the line layout of the poems on pages 71–3 and discuss what effect it has.

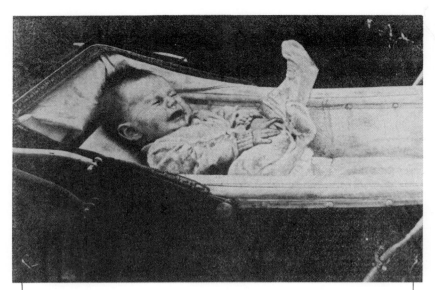

This is the child alone.

This is the child who cries for hours on end.

This is the child who is cold and unfed.

This is the child who is dull and lifeless.

This is the child in sodden clothes.

This is the child whose parents no longer have the will to cope.

This is the forgotten, the neglected child.

The NSPCC helps thousands of them every year, but there are thousands more who need our help and yours.

NSPCC. Neglect can scar for life.

For more information, write to: Neglect Campaign, Ref 71618, NSPCC, FREEPOST, London EC1B 1QQ **NSPCC**

This advertisement for the NSPCC reads like a free verse poem. In what ways is it like a poem? Write your own free verse poem using the same pattern, i.e. 'This is the . . .'.

BEGGAR

Beggar,
There he stoops all day,
Wrinkled,
Grey-haired,
Senile,
With his stained beard, and his pavement bowl,
Hand hopefully outstretched,
Entreating,
Entreating with his eyes,
Entreating with his tongue,
Entreating with his hand.

Yet we saunter by,
Eyes earthwards riveted.

Sometimes a gnarled stick,
Sometimes none,
Always the filthy *kanzu*,
The tattered *kanzu*,
We have observed him sightless,
Deaf and dumb,
We have seen him piteously, hopping
Hobbling and crawling.
Still we ignore the gnarled palm,
Still we pore over the drab pavement.

Perhaps he is blind
Pitiful
Yet he misses not every proffered coin
Though the gesture is silent.

Perhaps he can see?

So we stalk past.

A Kassam

75

DOWN AND OUT

Dark freezing nights
The stench of rotting food and cheap spirits
Churning my stomach
With disgust
And pity
And anger at myself
Because I turn away.

I want to get on with my life
My bright future
But in the dark and endless present
These half-humans
Huddle round a smoky fire
But feel no warmth.

Dustbins are their larders
Cardboard boxes
Like the one our new TV came in
Are their only beds

I hurry home
And shut the door with relief
But its no good
I can't shut out that sight.

Sarah Francis, aged 15

THE COMMISSION

In this poem there is a table
Groaning with food.
There is also a child
Groaning for lack of food.
The food is beautifully photographed
The meat more succulent
The fruit as juicy
As you are likely to see.
(The child is sketched in lightly
She is not important.)
The photograph is to be used
In a glossy magazine
As part of a campaign
Advertising after-dinner mints.

This evening the photographer
In receipt of his fee
Celebrates by dining with friends
In a famous West End restaurant.
Doodling on the napkin between courses
The photographer, always creative,
Draws a little Asian girl,
Naked, wide-eyed, pleading.
The photographer is pleased.
He has an idea for the next commission,
The one for famine relief.
The tandoori arrives
He puts away his pen
And picks up a fork.

Roger McGough

MONEY

Money is power: so said one.
Money is a cushion: so said another.
Money is the root of evil: so said still another.
Money means freedom: so runs an old saying.

And money is all of these – and more.
Money pays for whatever you want – if
    you have the money.
Money buys food, clothes, houses, land, guns,
    jewels, men, women, time to be lazy
    and listen to music.
Money buys everything except love, personality
    freedom, immortality, silence, peace.

Carl Sandburg

MONEY-MADNESS

Money is our madness, our vast collective madness.

And of course, if the multitude is mad
the individual carries his own grain of insanity around with him.

I doubt if any man living hands out a pound note without a pang;
and a real tremor, if he hands out a ten-pound note.

We quail, money makes us quail.
It has got us down, we grovel before it in strange terror.
And no wonder, for money has a fearful cruel power among men.

But it is not money we are so terrified of,
it is the collective money-madness of mankind.
For mankind says with one voice: How much is he worth?
Has he no money? Then let him eat dirt, and go cold. –

And if I have no money, they will give me a little bread
so I do not die,
but they will make me eat dirt with it.
I shall have to eat dirt, I shall have to eat dirt
if I have no money.

It is that that I am frightened of.
And that fear can become a delirium.
It is fear of my money-mad fellow-men.

We must have some money
to save us from eating dirt.

And this is all wrong.

Bread should be free,
shelter should be free,
fire should be free
to all and anybody, all and anybody, all over the world.

We must regain our sanity about money
before we start killing one another about it.
It's one thing or the other.

D H Lawrence

Over to You

The freedom of free verse means that it is easy and enjoyable to write. Write some free verse poems using the poems in this chapter for ideas.

Write about one of the poems in this chapter. 'Beggar', 'The Commission' and 'Money-Madness' are particularly suitable for this.

- Begin with an introduction saying simply and clearly what the poem is about.

- Discuss the ideas, the 'message' in the poem.

- Explain how free verse has been used by the poet to express this message.

- Conclude with a personal response, saying what you think of the poem, the ideas in it and the way they are expressed.

Browse through some magazines and see if you can find examples of the kind of contrast Roger McGough wrote about, for example glossy advertisements for luxury goods next to articles about poverty or suffering. Cut out and mount the photographs and write a personal response to them in prose or poetry.

Diversions

This poem has been turned into a riddle simply by removing the title. Read it carefully, then try to answer the questions on page 80. They will be easy if you have solved the riddle, but almost impossible if you haven't!

You hosts are almost glad he gate-crashed: see,
How his eyes brighten on the whisky, how his wit
Tumbles the company like a lightening stroke, –
You marvel where he gets his energy from . . .

But that same instant, here, far underground,
This fusty carcass stirs its shroud and swells.

'Stop, stop, oh for God's sake, stop!' you shriek
As your tears run down, but he goes on and on
Mercilessly till you think your ribs must crack . . .

While this carcass's eyes grimace, stitched
In the cramp of an ordeal, and a squeeze of blood
Crawls like scorpions into its hair.

You plead, limp, dangling in his mad voice, till
With a sudden blood-spittling cough, he chokes: he leaves
Trembling, soon after. You slump back down in a chair
Cold as a leaf, your heart scarcely moving . . .

Deep under the city's deepest stone
This grinning sack is bursting with your blood.

Ted Hughes

Who or what do you think the gate-crasher really is?

What is unusual about his behaviour and his approach to his victim? (Do not worry if you have no clue about the answer. Turn to page 166 and find out what the missing title is. It will make the poem easier to understand and should show you how important it is to pay attention to a poem's title.)

Make other riddles by finding suitable poems, copying them out without the title, and giving them to your friends to solve.

8 Words

Words dancin
words dancin
till dey sweat
words like fishes
jumpin out a net
words wild and free
joinin de poetry revelry
words back to back
words belly to belly

John Agard

Writers in English have a wider choice of words than writers in any other language – around 490,000, plus around 300,000 technical terms! Of course, there is a great deal of overlap, as we can see from this thesaurus entry for the word 'ship' (a thesaurus is a kind of dictionary which gives lists of synonyms – words of similar meaning – rather than definitions).

270 Ship
N. *ship*, vessel, boat, craft; bark, barque; great ship, little ship, cockleshell; bottom, keel, sail; hooker, tub, hull; hulk; Golden Hind; steamer, motor vessel; paddle steamer; passenger ship, liner, ocean greyhound, floating palace; channel steamer, ferry; hovercraft, hydrofoil; rotor ship; packet, dredger, hopper; transport, hospital ship; tender, escort vessel; pilot vessel; tug, launch; lightship, weather ship; underwater craft, submarine, U-boat, *warship.*
galley; pirate ship, privateer, corsair; Viking ship, longship; trireme
merchant ship, merchantman; cog, galleon; banana boat, tea clipper; slave ship, slaver; cargo boat, freighter, tramp; coaster; lugger; collier, tanker.
fishing boat, fishing smack, hooker; drifter, trawler; factory ship; whaler.
sailing ship, sailing boat; windjammer, clipper; tall ship; barque; brig, brigantine, schooner; frigate, corvette, *warship*; cutter, sloop, ketch, yawl; wherry; yacht, sailing dinghy, smack; dhow, junk, sampan.
boat, skiff; lifeboat; tender, dinghy, pram; longboat, jolly boat; cutter, gig; surf boat; barge, lighter, pontoon; ferry; houseboat; tugboat, tug; powerboat, motorboat, motor launch; cabin cruiser.
rowing boat, galley; eight, shell; skiff, dinghy, rubber dinghy; coracle; punt, gondola; canoe, outrigger, dugout; kayak.
raft, balsa, catamaran, trimaran; float, pontoon.

With so many words to choose from writers can express themselves very precisely by using the one which has exactly the right shade of meaning. In a story about an English merchant ship being attacked by a German submarine in the Second World War, for example, the word 'U-boat' would be more precise than 'submarine', and more authentic.

The prose writer is usually concerned only with a word's meaning, but the poet is interested in its sound as well, which may be used for rhyme, rhythm or other effects.

Here are some examples which show how a poet's choice of words (or *diction*) has been used to create an effect. The first of these shows how John Masefield made use of the sense, sounds and associations of some of the synonyms for 'ship'.

CARGOES

Quinquereme of Nineveh from distant Ophir
Rowing home to haven in sunny Palestine,
With a cargo of ivory,
And apes and peacocks,
Sandalwood, cedarwood, and sweet white wine.

Stately Spanish galleon coming from the Isthmus,
Dipping through the Tropics by the palm-green shores,
With a cargo of diamonds,
Emeralds, amethysts,
Topazes, and cinnamon, and gold moidores.

Dirty British coaster with a salt-caked smoke stack
Butting through the Channel in the mad March days,
With a cargo of Tyne coal,
Road-rail, pig-lead,
Firewood, iron-ware, and cheap tin trays.

John Masefield

Pick out the words in 'Cargoes' which suggest the beautiful, luxurious and exotic. Pick out the words which suggest cheapness, industry and dirt. What contrast between our civilisation and earlier civilisations is John Masefield pointing out? How does his use of words help him to do this?

THE CONVERGENCE OF THE TWAIN
(*Lines on the Loss of the "Titanic"*)

I

In a solitude of the sea
Deep from human vanity,
And the Pride of Life that planned her, stilly couches she.

II

Steel chambers, late the pyres
Of her salamandrine fires,
Cold currents thrid, and turn to rhythmic tidal lyres.

III

Over the mirrors meant
To glass the opulent
The sea-worm crawls – grotesque, slimed, dumb, indifferent.

IV

Jewels in joy designed
To ravish the sensuous mind
Lie lightless, all their sparkles bleared and black and blind.

V

Dim moon-eyed fishes near
Gaze at the gilded gear
And query: 'What does this vaingloriousness down here?' . . .

VI

Well: while was fashioning
This creature of cleaving wing,
The Immanent Will that stirs and urges everything

VII

Prepared a sinister mate
For her – so gaily great –
A shape of ice, for the time far and dissociate.

VIII

And as the smart ship grew
In stature, grace, and hue,
In shadowy silent distance grew the Iceberg too.

IX

Alien they seemed to be:
No mortal eye could see
The intimate welding of their later history,

X

Or sign that they were bent
By paths coincident
On being anon twin halves of one august event,

XI

Till the Spinner of the Years
Said "Now!" And each one hears,
And consummation comes, and jars two hemispheres.

Thomas Hardy

Pick out the words in this poem which bring out the majesty and beauty of the *Titanic*, and the words which bring out the horrors of her fate. Look particularly for places where these words create a powerful contrast.

BUBBLES

So fragile is the spherical, transparent shape
Of the ephemeral bubble.
So many glistening
As they cascade into each other.
The distorted reflection of our bodies
As we reach to snatch them.
The iridescent sheen of the gossamer
glinting bubbles.
They shine and glint
Until the surface
being damaged
Makes a pop!
All beauty lost
And vanished out of sight.

Martin Benbrook, aged 14

UPON JULIA'S CLOTHES

Whenas in silks my Julia goes,
Then, then, methinks, how sweetly flows
That liquefaction of her clothes!

Next, when I cast mine eyes and see
That brave vibration each way free,
– O how that glittering taketh me!

Robert Herrick

THE WINDHOVER

To Christ our Lord

I caught this morning morning's minion, king-
dom of daylight's dauphin, dapple-dawn-drawn Falcon, in his riding
Of the rolling level underneath him steady air, and striding
High there, how he rung upon the rein of a wimpling wing
In his ecstasy! then off, off forth on swing,
As a skate's heel sweeps smooth on a bow-bend: the hurl and gliding
Rebuffed the big wind. My heart in hiding
Stirred for a bird, – the achieve of, the mastery of the thing!

Brute beauty and valour and act, oh, air, pride, plume, here
Buckle! AND the fire that breaks from thee then, a billion
Times told lovelier, more dangerous, O my chevalier!

No wonder of it: shéer plód makes plough down sillion
Shine, and blue-bleak embers, ah my dear,
Fall, gall themselves, and gash gold-vermilion.

Gerard Manley Hopkins

Pick out the words in these three poems that bring out the beauty of the everyday things they describe.

85

BROOKLYN COP

Built like a gorilla, but less timid,
Thick-fleshed, steak-coloured, with two
Hieroglyphs in his face that mean
Trouble, he walks the sidewalk and the
Thin tissue over violence. This morning,
When he said 'See you, babe' to his wife,
He hoped it, he truly hoped it,
He is a gorilla
To whom, 'hiya honey' is no cliche.

Should the tissue tear, should he plunge through
Into violence, what clubbings, what
Gunshots between Phoebe's,
Whamburger and Louie's Place.

Who would be him, gorilla with a nightstick
Whose home is a place
He might, this time, never get back to.

And who would be who have to be
    His victims?

                    Norman MacCaig

EXECUTIVE

I am a young executive. No cuffs than mine are cleaner;
I have a Slimline briefcase and I use the firm's Cortina.
In every roadside hostelry from here to Burgess Hill
The *maîtres d' hôtel* all know me well and let me sign the bill.

You ask me what it is I do. Well actually, you know,
I'm partly a liaison man and partly P.R.O.
Essentially I integrate the current export drive
And basically I'm viable from ten o'clock till five.

For vital off-the-record work – that's talking transport-wise –
I've a scarlet Aston-Martin – and does she go? She flies!
Pedestrians and dogs and cats – we mark them down for slaughter.
I also own a speed-boat which has never touched the water.

She's built of fibre-glass, of course. I call her 'Mandy Jane'
After a bird I used to know – No soda, please, just plain –
And how did I acquire her? Well to tell you about that
And to put you in the picture I must wear my other hat.

I do some mild developing. The sort of place I need
Is a quiet country market town that's rather run to seed.
A luncheon and a drink or two, a little *savoir faire* –
I fix the Planning Officer, the Town Clerk and the Mayor.

And if some preservationist attempts to interfere
A 'dangerous structure' notice from the Borough Engineer
Will settle any buildings that are standing in our way –
The modern style, sir, with respect, has really come to stay.

John Betjeman

Which words help to build up a picture of the 'Brooklyn Cop' and the 'Executive'?

Which words add authenticity to the description of their work?

What words might the preservationist in 'Executive' use to describe the 'dangerous structure'? Why is this difference in choice of words crucial? What will the words 'dangerous structure' enable the executive to do?

Jargon

Most types of work have their own specialist technical terms. When these terms are used too frequently to an audience who do not understand them they are dismissed as *jargon*. Journalists are particularly prone to lapse into jargon since they work with words. Often, particularly when under pressure, it is easier to cobble together some bits of journalistic jargon than to struggle to find more precise words. Here is an argument on this subject between the British poet Robert Graves and a New York critical weekly (a weekly journal of literary reviews):

TILTH

Robert Graves, the British veteran, is no longer in the poetic swim. He still resorts to traditional metres and rhyme, and to such outdated words as *tilth*; witholding his 100% approbation also from contemporary poems that favour sexual freedom.

From a New York critical weekly

Gone are the drab monosyllabic days
When "agricultural labour" still was *tilth*;
And "100% approbation", *praise*;
And "pornographic modernism", *filth* –
Yet still I stand by *tilth* and *filth* and *praise*.

Robert Graves

What criticism does the New York critical weekly make of Robert Graves' diction? How does Robert Graves defend his use of words and at the same time criticise those used by the New York critical weekly? How does his use of verse strengthen his argument? Who do you think has won the argument and why?

You can explore journalistic jargon further in the poster (opposite) which was found in the newsroom of the BBC. Of course, its message is ironic: by highlighting a range of jargon and cliché, it aimed to embarrass journalists into thinking of fresh expressions.

THE JOURNALISTS' JARGON GENERATOR

Stuck for a meaningful concept? Don't waste time thinking, just combine words from the columns below and create a really attention-grabbing article. Yes, using the jargon generator, you too could come up with something as penetrating as 'across the board industrial negotiating machinery is balanced on a knife edge' or 'meaningful media watchdog is getting off the ground'.

across the board	copycat	breakthrough
bitter	Euro-	charter
in-depth	fact-finding	clash
inflationary	grass-roots	cut
low-key	high street bank	negotiating machinery
meaningful	industrial	probe
ongoing	interest rates	saga
overwhelming	kiss-and-tell	shock
penetrating	media	walkabout
plummeting	ministerial	walkout
swingeing	Stock Exchange	watchdog
very real	unemployment	whitewash

is alive and well	laid off
and that's official!	of many years standing
is like a hole in the head	is getting off the ground
is balanced on a knife edge	since records began
is bending over backwards	hands are tied
is bowing out	is keeping a finger on the pulse

Over to You

Write about one of the poems, or group of poems, in this chapter. Use or adapt this plan as you wish:

- Explain what the poet is saying.

- Examine how it is said: What form has been used? If it is free verse, what effect has the layout of the lines? If it is rhymed metrical verse, how have rhyme and rhythm been used? Give particular attention to the poet's use of words. Comment on any other points of interest.

- Write your response to the ideas in the poem and the way they have been expressed.

Use the thesaurus entry to pick out some other interesting synonyms for 'ship' and use them to write more verses for Masefield's poem, or to write your own poem if you prefer.

Write two letters to a newspaper, one giving reasons why an interesting old building should be preserved, another giving reasons why it should be pulled down. Choose your words carefully so that they cast different interpretations on the facts.

Use the 'Journalists' Jargon Generator' to write a poem or a sensationalised newspaper article.

Diversions

The Church has a problem with words. Old-fashioned words like 'thee' and 'brethren' give the impression that the Church is out of date. This has been partly put right by the many modern translations of the Bible now available. However, it is less easy to modernise the hymns! Changing a word often affects the rhythm or rhyme, which means that a whole line or verse has to be rewritten.

Here is the original version of a well-known hymn. Read it carefully making a mental note of any old-fashioned words, and then try to modernise it. Your version must rhyme, and the rhythm must be correct or it will not fit the tune! When you have finished compare your version with the one written for *Hymns for Today's Church* which you will find on page 166. Finally, discuss the advantages and disadvantages of modernising hymns in this way.

> **While shepherds watched their flocks by night,**
> **All seated on the ground,**
> **The angel of the Lord came down,**
> **And glory shone around.**

'Fear not,' said he (for mighty dread
  Had seized their troubled mind);
'Glad tidings of great joy I bring
  To you and all mankind.

'To you in David's town this day
  Is born of David's line
A Saviour, who is Christ the Lord;
  And this shall be the sign:

'The heavenly Babe you there shall find
  To human view displayed,
All meanly wrapped in swathing bands,
  And in a manger laid.'

thus spake the seraph; and forthwith
  Appeared a shining throng
Of angels praising God, who thus
  Addressed their joyful song:

'All glory be to God on high,
  And to the earth be peace;
Good will henceforth from heaven to men
  Begin and never cease.'

N Tate

9 *Wordplay*

What do you call a vicar's budgie?
A bird of pray!

This joke plays upon the double meaning 'pray/prey' – a kind of wordplay called the *pun*. Many other types are possible including the jumbling up of words and letters, and using the sound of words for special effects such as *alliteration* and *onomatopoeia*.

The Pun

The pun is the commonest form of wordplay, as these varied examples show. It is particularly effective for humour, but can also be used in serious writing.

THE SONG OF THE DUMB WAITER

Who went to sleep in the flower-bed?
Who let the fire-dog out of the shed?

Who sailed the sauce-boat down the stream?
What did the railway-sleeper dream?

Who was it chopped the boot-tree down,
And rode the clothes-horse through the town?

James Reeves

SEA'S CAPE

I
see
gulls
Icy
gulls
I see
gulls screaming
– Aye –
I see seagulls
screaming, see
Ai YUY –
scream

. . . 'Ice *CREAM*'
the seagulls
seem to scream
Hi Hi *eee*
Ye – Icy seagulls!

   see
Gulls   see
eyes

cream

Michael Horovitz

An Ear passed me
the other day
And silently
went on its way

I wonder who
that ear can be
And has it ever
heard of me.

Spike Milligan

Can you spot the double meaning
in this 'visual pun'?

The epitaph below shows that the pun can be used equally effectively to make a serious point. It is very cleverly written. Study it and explain how it works.

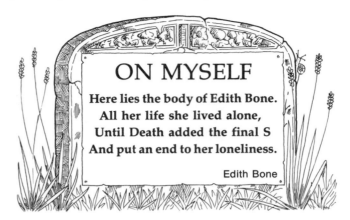

ON MYSELF

Here lies the body of Edith Bone.
All her life she lived alone,
Until Death added the final S
And put an end to her loneliness.

Edith Bone

How many puns can you find in the newspaper cuttings? Explain both senses of the double meanings.

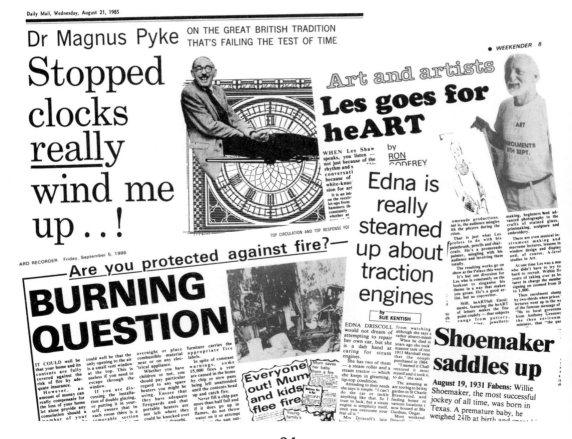

Word-Jumbling

This can be done in many different ways. Here are two interesting examples. Note how Roger McGough plays on the word 'bat' and combines it with other words. Sir J C Squire takes word-jumbling even further – almost to the point of nonsense. Why is this appropriate to the subject of the poem?

GOODBAT NIGHTMAN

God bless all policemen
and fighters of crime,
May thieves go to jail
for a very long time.

They've had a hard day
helping clean up the town,
Now they hang from the mantelpiece
both upside down.

A glass of warm blood
and then straight up the stairs,
Batman and Robin
are saying their prayers.

* * *

They've locked all the doors
and they've put out the bat,
Put on their batjamas
(They like doing that)

They've filled their batwater-bottles
made their batbeds,
With two springy battresses
for sleepy batheads.

They're closing red eyes
and they're counting black sheep,
Batman and Robin
are falling asleep.

Roger McGough

95

BALLADE OF SOPORIFIC ABSORPTION

Ho! Ho! Yes! Yes! It's very all well,
    You may drunk I am think, but I tell you I'm not,
I'm as sound as a fiddle and fit as a bell,
    And stable quite ill to see what's what.
    I under *do* stand you surprise a got
When I headed my smear with gooseberry jam:
    And I've swallowed, I grant, a beer of lot –
But I'm not so think as you drunk I am.

Can I liquor my stand? Why, yes, like hell!
    I care not how many a tossed I've pot
I shall stralk quite weight and not yutter an ell,
    my feech will not spalter the least little jot:
    If you knownly had own! – well, I gave him a dot,
And I said to him, 'Sergeant, I'll come like a lamb –
    The floor it seems like a storm in a yacht,
But I'm not so think as you drunk I am.'

For example, to prove it I'll tale you a tell –
    I once knew a fellow named Apricot –
I'm sorry, I just chair over a fell –
    A trifle – this chap, on a very day hot –
    If I hadn't consumed that last whisky of tot! –
As I said now, this fellow, called Abraham –

    Ah? One more? Since it's you! Just a do me will spot –
but I'm not so think as you drunk I am.

ENVOI

So, Prince, you suggest I've bolted my shot?
Well, like what you say, and soul your damn!
    I'm an upple litset by the talk you rot –
But I'm not so think as you drunk I am.

Sir J C Squire

96

Alliteration

Alliteration could be called the opposite of rhyme – it occurs when words *begin* with the same sound. In Old English poetry it was used instead of rhyme, and though it has lost that privileged position it is still widely used today.

TWO ANGLO-SAXON RIDDLES

I heard of a wonder, of words moth-eaten;
that is a strange thing, I thought, wierd
that a man's song be swallowed by a worm,
his binded sentences, his bedside stand-by
rustled in the night – and the robber guest
not one whit the wiser for the words he had mumbled.

The wave, over the wave, a wierd thing I saw,
thorough-wrought, and wonderfully ornate:
a wonder on the wave – water became bone.

Copy out one of the riddles above and underline the letters which alliterate – then try and solve it (the answers may be found on page 166).

From THE BATTLE OF MALDON (fought in 991)

Flashed a dart from Danish hand,
fist-driven, and flew too truly,
bit the Earl, Aethelred's thane.
There stood at his side a stripling warrior,
young Wulfmaer, Wulfstan's son,
fresh to the field. In a flash he
plucked from its place the blood-black point,
flung back the filed spear; again it flew.
Home sank the steel, stretched on the plain
him so who late had pierced the Prince so grievously.

Which words are emphasised by alliteration? Why are these words particularly important?

Compare the use of alliteration in Old English poetry with its use in a modern poem. Note how the alliteration emphasises the secretary's bitterness:

REVERIE FOR A SECRETARY

Feeling fragile and incredibly bored I listen to my boss
saying he takes five newspapers to get other viewpoints
from which he makes up his mind on world events.
I give him my look of awe thinking,
well bully for you, with a brain like that
you are paid nine times more than me?
Over his head and through the window
the sky is blue and beckoning. I wish I had wings.
'The return on capital investment is up two per cent'
Dear God, who really cares?
Wouldn't we be happier making daisy chains?
How disgustingly fat he is.
His hair parting would just fit an axe.
I am not brave. I can't walk out
leaving a question mark in the air.
I am your natural serving maid
dropping curtseys to the gentry.

Those figures are not correct?
How would you know?
You can only just crayon picture books.
He must know these figures came from the computer
and he supplied the original figures.
I could walk up and wack him over the head
with that dictaphone he can't use,
then drag him and push him out of the window.
From seventeen storeys he would splash.
Suicide while the balance of his pea brain was disturbed.
Mercy killer breaks down in dock.
Blond in penthouse drama.
He is looking at my legs and breathing through his nose.
Now he will ask about my boyfriend.
Here it comes right on cue.
'Yes, we went dancing last night.'
Stark naked and I gave myself to fifteen rugger players.
Should I tear off my clothes and scream rape?
They wouldn't believe me. They say he is one of those.
And now he wants a cup of coffee.
That's his seventh and he hasn't been to the loo.
My cool lily white hands deftly serve him
and my beautiful body glides round his desk.
My cool lily white hands want to pour it in his ear
and my beautiful body wants to dance as he screams.
He has hairs growing out of his nose.
I never noticed them before, and he reeks
of that lousy after shave lotion, yecch,
he doesn't even smell like a man.
Now he is going to lunch. Listen to him wheeze and puff.
'You will be back at three Mr Chatterton?'
Smile you bitch smile. He is bound to have a coronary
carrying all that blubber about.
Oh mummy, for this you made me do my homework?

Stella Coulson

The examples below show that alliteration certainly adds punch to a headline! Pick up almost any daily paper and you will find dozens of similar examples – watch out for alliteration in advertisements too.

Classroom chaos call

By ELAINE COOPER

A SERIES of one-day could bring chaos to schools in the area

Postcard postscript to the big pier prang

A COMPLETE pictorial record of Southend Pier's latest calamity — when a 600-ton motor tank... ...ed making a hole near pier agreed by local

THE STAR SAYS

Sinister side of secrecy

THREE months after Deputy Chief Constable John Stalker was t on a mission to the Western

Pupils are on parade

WELCOME to Westminster IM...

Business boost for students

A NEW Educational Initiative for Young People is to be launched by the West Yorkshire

Widow slams DHSS officials

'Heartless and humiliating'

SOUTHEND'S social security office has been branded heartless and humiliating by a recently widowed young woman.
She says she suffered

had die... nesday.

...mething about the food

April 19. She and the husband set up home

Vandal victim

FURIOUS shopkeeper Nick Leppert finally snapped after the use of...

Tools of trade

Winter warmers for wet weather

Onomatopoeia

Sometimes poets use the sounds of words to suggest the things they refer to, as in this example:

THE EXPRESS

Slowly she slides from the station,
Safety valves hissing, pistons sliding,
Clattering over the cluttered trackwork
Fretting for the main line's freedom . . .

Study it for a moment: Which sounds in the first two lines suggest the sounds of a steam engine? Which sounds in the third line suggest a train rattling over points? Got the idea? Now try to complete the poem using onomatopoeia to suggest the sound of the whistle, the drumming of the wheels, the train going under a bridge, etc. When you have finished compare what you have written with Stephen Spender's poem on the same subject:

101

THE EXPRESS

After the first powerful plain manifesto
The black statement of pistons, without more fuss
But gliding like a queen, she leaves the station.
Without bowing and with restrained unconcern
She passes the houses which humbly crowd outside,
The gasworks and at last the heavy page
Of death, printed by gravestones in the cemetery.
Beyond the town there lies the open country
Where, gathering speed, she acquires mystery,
The luminous self-possession of ships on ocean.
It is now she begins to sing – at first quite low
Then loud, and at last with a jazzy madness –
The song of her whistle screaming at curves,
Of deafening tunnels, brakes, innumerable bolts.
And always light, aerial, underneath
Goes the elate metre of her wheels.
Steaming through metal landscape on her lines
She plunges new eras of wild happiness
Where speed throws up strange shapes, broad curves
And parallels clean like the steel of guns.
At last, further than Edinburgh or Rome,
Beyond the crest of the world, she reaches night
Where only a low streamline brightness
Of phosphorous on the tossing hills is white.
Ah, like a comet through flame she moves entranced
Wrapt in her music no bird song, no, nor bough
Breaking with honey buds, shall ever equal.

Stephen Spender

In 'The Last Laugh', Wilfred Owen uses onomatopoeia to suggest the sounds of war:

THE LAST LAUGH

'O Jesus Christ! I'm hit,' he said; and died.
Whether he vainly cursed, or prayed indeed,
The Bullets chirped – In vain! vain! vain!
Machine-guns chuckled, – Tut-tut! Tut-tut!
And the Big Gun guffawed.

Another sighed, – 'O Mother, mother! Dad!'
Then smiled, at nothing, childlike, being dead.
  And the lofty Shrapnel-cloud
  Leisurely gestured, – Fool!
  And the falling splinters tittered.

'My Love!' one moaned. Love-languid seemed his mood,
Till slowly lowered, his whole face kissed the mud.
  And the Bayonets' long teeth grinned;
  Rabbles of Shells hooted and groaned;
  And the Gas hissed.

Wilfred Owen

Compare the horrors of war described in this poem with those of over a thousand years ago described in the extract from 'The Battle of Maldon' on page 97.

Over to You

Make a collection of jokes, seaside postcards, newspaper cuttings, poems, etc., which use wordplay. Explain how each example works.

Make up some jokes, slogans and poems using different types of wordplay.

Write in detail about some of the poems in this chapter. Discuss all the aspects of poetry that you have covered so far and pay particular attention to wordplay.

Diversions

Write punning captions for these seaside postcards.

The original captions may be found on page 166.

10 Feeling

Poetry is the spontaneous overflow of powerful feelings: it takes its origins from emotion recollected in tranquillity.

William Wordsworth

Feelings are powerful things, so powerful that they are frequently stronger than reason – as anyone who has ever fallen in love will know! Our feelings can help us to understood other people – in the words of a common saying we 'feel for them', particularly when they are suffering. In this way our feelings can make us better and more humane people. However, because feelings are so powerful, it is important that we learn to distinguish between the true and the false if we are to avoid being deceived – either in literature or real life! One form of false feeling sometimes found in second-rate novels and verse is sentimentality – a faked rather than genuine form of emotion.

Poetry, in the hands of a first-rate poet, is a particularly effective way of expressing feelings. Sometimes it takes more than the plain facts to get an idea across. Readers have to be made to *feel* it in their hearts, rather than just understand it in their heads – this is something that poetry is well suited to.

Read the following poems about children and childhood quietly to youself, taking note of how each one made you feel. Note that an example of second-rate sentimental verse has been slipped in among them. How easily can you pick it out?

105

DEATH OF A CAT

I rose early
On the fourth day
Of his illness,
And went downstairs
To see if he was
All right.

He was not in the
House, and I rushed
Wildly round the
Garden calling his name.

I found him lying
Under a rhododendron
Bush,
His black fur
Wet, and matted
With the dew.

I knelt down beside him.
And he opened his
Mouth as if to
Miaow
But no sound came.

I picked him up
And he lay quietly
In my arms
As I carried him
Indoors.

Suddenly he gave
A quiet miaow
And I felt his body tense,
And then lie still.

I laid his warm,
Lifeless body on
The floor, and
Rubbed my fingers
Through his fur.

A warm tear
Dribbled down
My cheek and
Left a salt taste
On my lips.

I stood up, and
Walked quietly
Out of the room.

Anthony Thompson

Anthony Thompson says very little about his own feelings yet manages to express them strongly, and evoke similar feelings in the reader. How does he do this?

106

A CASE OF MURDER

They should not have left him there alone,
Alone that is except for the cat.
He was only nine, not old enough
To be left alone in a basement flat,
Alone, that is, except for the cat.
A dog would have been a different thing,
A big gruff dog with slashing jaws,
But a cat with round eyes mad as gold,
Plump as a cushion with tucked-in paws –
Better have left him with a fair sized rat!
But what they did was leave him with a cat.
He hated that cat; he watched it sit,
A buzzing machine of soft black stuff,
He sat and watched and he hated it,
Snug in its fur, hot blood in a muff,
And its mad gold star and the way it sat
Crooning dark warmth: he loathed all that.
So he took Daddy's stick and he hit the cat.
Then quick as a sudden crack in glass
It hissed, black flash, to a hiding place
In the dust and dark beneath the couch,
And he followed the grin on his new-made face,
A wide-eyed, frightened snarl of a grin,
And he took the stick and he thrust it in,
Hard and quick in the furry dark.
The black fur squealed and he felt his skin
Prickle with sparks of dry delight.
Then the cat again came into sight,
Shot for the door that wasn't quite shut,
But the boy, quick too, slammed fast the door:
The cat, half-through, was cracked like a nut
And the soft black thud was dumped on the floor.
Then the boy was suddenly terrified
And he bit his knuckles and cried and cried;
But he had to so something with the dead thing there.
His eyes squeezed beads of salty prayer
But the wound of fear gaped wide and raw;
He dared not tough the thing with his hands
So he fetched a spade and shovelled it
And dumped the load of heavy fur
In the spidery cupboard under the stair
Where it's been for years, and though it died
It's grown in that cupboard and its hot low purr
Grows slowly louder year by year:
There'll not be a corner for the boy to hide
When the cupboard swells and all sides split
And the huge black cat pads out of it.

Vernon Scannell

107

Trace the development of the boy's feelings throughout 'A Case of Murder'. How did the poem make you feel? Compare the way feelings are presented in this poem with 'Death of a Cat'.

WHERE IS MY BOY TONIGHT?

Where is my wandering boy tonight –
The boy of my tenderest care,
The boy that was once my joy and light,
The child of my love and prayer?
My heart overflows, for I love him he knows,
Oh, where is my boy, where is he tonight?

Once he was pure as morning dew,
As he knelt at his mother's knee;
No face was so bright, no heart more true,
And none was so sweet as he.
My heart overflows, for I love him he knows,
Oh, where is my boy, where is he tonight?

Oh, could I see you now, my boy,
As fair as in olden time,
When prattle and smile made home a joy,
And life was a merry chime!
My heart overflows, for I love him he knows,
Oh, where is my boy, where is he tonight?

Go for my wandering boy tonight;
Go, search for him where you will;
But bring him to me with all his blight,
And tell him I love him still!
My heart overflows, for I love him he knows,
Oh, where is my boy, where is he tonight?

Tell him that Jesus loves him too,
And is waiting to bring him home;
He surely will yield to Love so true,
Oh, plead with him now to come!
My heart overflows, for I love him he knows,
Oh, where is my boy, where is he tonight?

R Lowry

108

In the following three poems descriptive details are used to create a mood and express feeling. Read each poem carefully and discuss how this is done.

A SUMMER STORM

A faint growl,
As clouds prowl the horizon.
The heavens close black, threatening curtains.
Birds disperse on silent wings,
To escape the coming onslaught.
The atmosphere becomes sticky.
Small drops of rain burst free from bulging clouds
And descend rapidly towards the waiting land.
A flash of light seems to crack the heavens open in a long, jagged blazing tear.
Invisible wind reaches out with icy fingers,
To lure defenceless rain to patter on cold glass.

Inside a small dark bedroom, hides a tearful child.
In bed, he sweats beneath heavy blankets,
Desperately fighting against the need to raise his head for a lungful of cold air.
Strange noises continue outside his room.
The house grows restless,
Creaking stairs and whispering voices,
The wind grows angry.
A bright flash lights the room.
The screech of a frightened cat
Competes with pounding rain.

A summer storm.

Joanne Eagle, aged 15

THE GRAVE
OF LITTLE SU

THE SON

Dew on the secret orchid
Like crying eyes.
No thing to bind the heart to.
Misted flowers I cannot bear to cut.
Grass like a cushion,
The pine like a parasol:
The wind is a skirt,
The waters are tinkling pendants.
A coach with lacquered sides
Waits for someone in the evening.
Cold blue candle-flames
Strain to shine bright.
Beneath West Mound
The wind puffs the rain.

Li Ho

Lying awake, in the room
over their room, the voices
drifting up through the floor-boards –
a grinding, night-long quarrel
between the two who made you.
How can you bear to listen?

A shared bed, a shared hatred
to warm it in the small hours.
Four living children, one dead.
Five proofs of something, one you
who lie there above them. Grey
coals hiss as the fire burns low.

Edward Lucie-Smith

'Quiet fun' and 'Kill the Children' both deal with violence, yet they evoke very different feelings. What are these feelings and how are they evoked?

QUIET FUN

My son Augustus, in the street, one day,
    Was feeling quite exceptionally merry.
A stranger asked him: 'Can you tell me, pray,
    The quickest way to Brompton Cemetery?'
'The quickest way? You bet I can!' said Gus,
    And pushed the fellow underneath a bus.

Whatever people say about my son,
    He does enjoy his little bit of fun.

Harry Graham

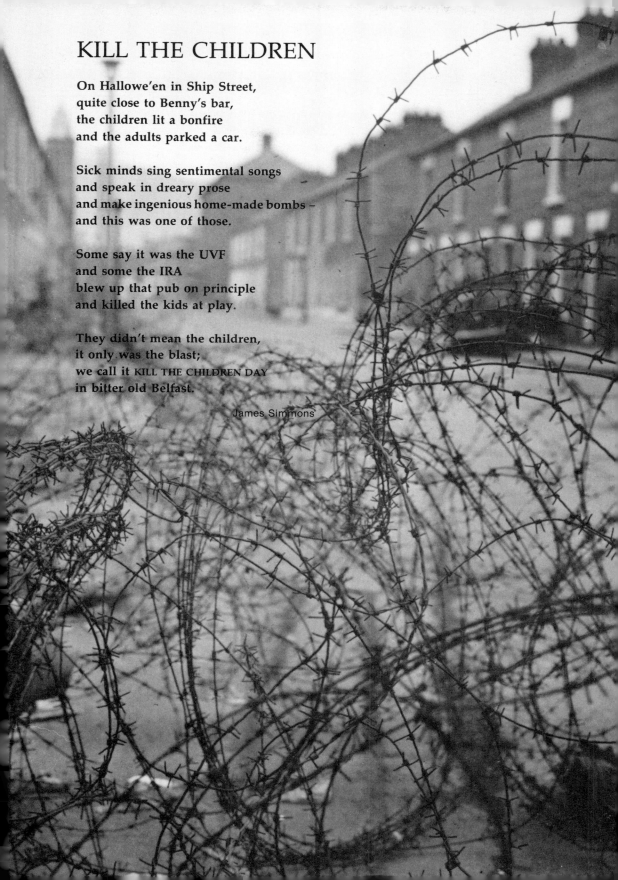

KILL THE CHILDREN

On Hallowe'en in Ship Street,
quite close to Benny's bar,
the children lit a bonfire
and the adults parked a car.

Sick minds sing sentimental songs
and speak in dreary prose
and make ingenious home-made bombs –
and this was one of those.

Some say it was the UVF
and some the IRA
blew up that pub on principle
and killed the kids at play.

They didn't mean the children,
it only was the blast;
we call it KILL THE CHILDREN DAY
in bitter old Belfast.

James Simmons

DISRUPTIVE MINORITY

Rude words on the blackboard,
Crushed chalk on the floor,
Books bunged out the window,
Run out, slam the door.

Teacher's depression
Me and my class.
Football in the playground
Connects with school glass.

Cigarettes in the toilet
And nudie books too.
When I leave this dump
Then what will I do?

I'm nothing special,
The school taught me that.
I haven't got brains
And my prospects are flat.

Can't hit back at the system
It's blank, has no features,
So while I'm at school
I'll take it out on the teachers.

Alan Gilbey

How does the boy in this poem feel? How do the teachers feel about him? What do you feel about this poem? Which side has your sympathy, and why?

Talking Point

Which poem in this chapter did you find sentimental? Which most moved you? Why?

Over to You

Choose one of the poems in this chapter and write in detail about the feelings it expresses and evokes. Use these questions as a guide:

- What does the writer feel about the subject of the poem?

- How has the writer tried to convey this feeling to you? Was he successful?

- What are the feelings of any characters in the poems – for example, the boy in 'Disruptive Minority'?

Write about other interesting features in the poem and conclude with a personal response.

Recall one of the most moving moments of your life and write a poem about it.

Diversions

In 1876 a train plummeted from the Ashtabula Railway Bridge in Ohio into the waters below with the loss of 85 lives including a well-known preacher named Philip Paul Bliss. This disaster moved Julia A Moore, America's worst poet, to write the following poem in which she tries to convey her feelings about the magnitude of the disaster and to evoke sympathy in her readers.

How does she fail? Try to do better by rewriting the poem.

THE ASHTABULA DISASTER

Have you heard of the dreadful fate
　　Of Mr. P. P. Bliss and wife?
Of their death I will relate,
　　And also others lost their life;
Ashtabula bridge disaster,
　　Where so many people died
Without a thought that destruction
　　Would plunge them 'neath the wheel of tide.

113

Chorus: Swiftly passed the engine's call,
    Hastening souls on to death,
Warning not one of them all;
    It brought despair right and left.

Among the ruins are many friends,
    Crushed to death amidst the roar,
On one thread all may depend,
    And hope they've reached the other shore.
P. P. Bliss showed great devotion
    To his faithful wife, his pride,
When he saw that she must perish
    He died a martyr by her side.

P. P. Bliss went home above –
    Left all friends, earth, and fame,
To rest in God's holy love;
    Left on earth his work and name.
The people love his work by numbers,
    It is read by great and small,
He by it will be remembered,
    He has left it for us all.

His good name from time to time
    Will rise on land and sea;
It is known in distant climes,
    Let it echo wide and free.
One good man among the number,
    Found sweet rest in a short time,
His weary soul may sweetly slumber
    Within the vale, heaven sublime.

Destruction lay on every side,
    Confusion, fire and despair;
No help, no hope, so they died,
    Two hundred people over there.
Many ties was there broken,
    Many a heart was filled with pain,
Each one left a little token,
    For above they live again.

Chorus: Swiftly passed the engine's call,
    Hastening souls on to death,
Warning not one of them all;
    It brought despair right and left.

Julia A Moore

11 *Irony*

irony, n. 1. use of words to mean the opposite of what is said. 2. event, situation opposite of that expected.

Collins Dictionary

If you broke a plate while helping with the washing-up, your parents might say 'You're a big help!' This is an example of *irony* in which the intended meaning is the opposite of what is said. This ironic comment can be more effective than saying 'Don't be so clumsy!' because it emphasises the contrast between what you have done, i.e. broken a plate, and what you should be doing, i.e. helping. It also contains an element of humour which helps to soften the criticism.

Irony can be used to express anything from the mild criticism of the above example to more severe criticism, anger or bitterness. Irony which is particularly bitter or scathing is called *sarcasm*.

SCHOOL TAUGHT ME

School taught me
to write my name
to recite the answers
to feel ashamed
to stand in corners
to wait in line
to kiss the rod

to be on time
and trust in God
To make me a model citizen
That was their goal
Well I don't know about that
But it was useful training
For a career on the dole.

Leon Rosselson

115

WINDSCALE

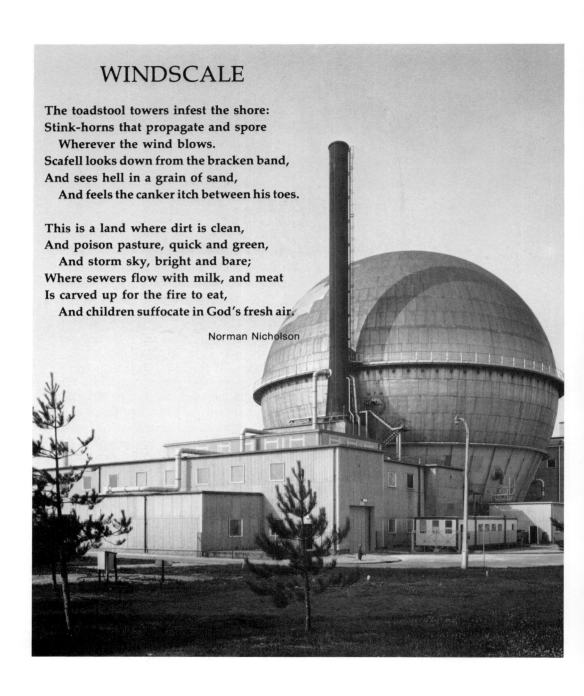

The toadstool towers infest the shore:
Stink-horns that propagate and spore
   Wherever the wind blows.
Scafell looks down from the bracken band,
And sees hell in a grain of sand,
   And feels the canker itch between his toes.

This is a land where dirt is clean,
And poison pasture, quick and green,
   And storm sky, bright and bare;
Where sewers flow with milk, and meat
Is carved up for the fire to eat,
   And children suffocate in God's fresh air.

Norman Nicholson

Notice how both these poems use rhyme to reinforce the irony.

Verse two of 'Windscale' is full of ironic contrasts. Explain the cause of these apparent contradictions. What message is the irony used to communicate?

116

WAGES

The wages of work is cash.
The wages of cash is want more cash.
The wages of want more cash is vicious competition.
The wages of vicious competition is – the world we live in.

The work-cash-want circle is the viciousest circle
that ever turned men into fiends.

Earning a wage is a prison occupation
and a wage-earner is a sort of gaol-bird.
Earning a salary is a prison overseer's job,
a gaoler instead of a gaol-bird.

Living on your income is strolling grandly outside the prison
in terror lest you have to go in. And since the work-prison covers
almost every scrap of the living earth, you stroll up and down
on a narrow beat, about the same as a prisoner taking his exercise.

This is called universal freedom.

D H Lawrence

FOODLESS CHILDREN

Foodless Children,
With stomachs puffed out,
Why have you no food to eat?
Why do you beg?

Foodless Children,
Suffering from starvation,
Why is your skin like paper?
Why do your bones poke out?

Foodless Children,
Eaten up by disease,
Why not see a doctor?
Why not?

Foodless Children,
You are so thin,
Your eyes are so appealing,
And you will soon be dead.

Maldwyn Davies

What is ironic about the questions in 'Foodless Children'?

THE HERO

The elegant body shivers with anticipation
As the greyhound stands poised behind the line
Its mouth caged like a prisoner behind bars.
    They're off!
The Hare rattles at the side of the track
The greyhounds' lunging legs blur in pursuit.
People scream and shout. The pace increases.
Dogs swerve around the corner like braking cars.
The Hare halts: the dogs skid.
People close in like an army around the winner.
Cameras flash, champagne flows
As the winner is bundled into a car –
A forgotten hero,
Locked away
Until next time.

Samantha King, aged 15

BADGER

Harmless they call him, a lovable nocturnal thing,
a family man spending daylight in his deep sett.
He has an old reputation for remaining aloof.
I thought he stuffed himself on insects and roots,
a fallen egg, a few mice, nothing his own size.
But from a cable-drum he came sniffing for our buck
after dark, baiting him and scratching at the mesh,
then deadly serious one night with his big jaws
and his bone-crushing molars rampant.
He wanted much more than a boring vegetable dish.

Grizzled snouter with claws and thick white stripe,
he scooped a hole under the boxwood hutch,
splintered the floor with his ramming head
and then clambered up and through it.
Our poor young rabbit must have died of fright
but not before the badger minced him
into string and slippery pulp.
That lovable thing left a smear of blood and droppings
on a mile-long strip of hutch and run
before a smallholder blew his head off.

John Tripp

What ironic contrasts are presented in 'The Hero' and 'Badger'?

118

ASSAULT

Gas!
faces turned,
eyes scanned the sky,
hands feverishly ripped open canisters,
and masks were soon covering faces.
A man choked
as the white cloud,
swirling round him like fog, caught him
unawares.
Then his body flopped over.
Shells floated across
as if suspended by hidden strings,
and then, tired,
they sank earthwards.

A command!
I fixed my bayonet,
scrambled over the open trench
and struggled through
the thick pasty mud.

It was quiet
as we walked
except for the sucking,
groaning, squelching sound
which came from the wet earth
as it tried
to creep into our stockings.
The wind cut me.

Over the wall!
Then a whistle.
'Good luck, mates.'
Mind that hole. Through the wire.
Over the top.
And kill.
'God. This is fun!'

Erno Muller

How can you tell that the last line of 'Assault' is not an expression of enjoyment, but is meant to be ironic?

BASE DETAILS

If I were fierce, and bald, and short of breath,
I'd live with scarlet Majors at the Base,
And speed glum heroes up the line to death.
You'd see me with my puffy petulant face,
Guzzling and gulping in the best hotel,
Reading the Roll of Honour. 'Poor young chap,'
I'd say – 'I used to know his father well;
Yes, we've lost heavily in this last scrap.'
And when the war is done and youth stone dead,
I'd toddle safely home and die – in bed.

Siegfried Sassoon

Over to You

Jot down and discuss some of the ironic comments you have heard in everyday life, for example, a father to his son who arrives home wearing an earring, 'Very pretty, why don't you have a ring through your nose as well?'.

Think of an ironic twist of fate, a poor man inheriting a fortune just before he died, for example, and write a story or poem about it.

Try to rewrite some of the poems in this chapter in a way that expresses the same message without using irony – is it possible?

Bearing the last exercise in mind, write about some of the poems explaining how irony is essential to the way the poet's message is expressed. Do not forget to comment on other interesting aspects of the poems and to conclude with a personal response to the ideas in the poems and the way they are expressed.

Diversions

A highly effective way of expressing anger or disagreement is to use humour as a weapon rather than to attack directly. One way to do this is to write a *parody*. A parody is a humorous or ironic version of a well-known piece which highlights the points you wish to attack.

This parody of a well-known hymn was written to attack the ideas of the controversial Bishop of Durham.

57 ALL THINGS BRIGHT AND BEAUTIFUL

Chorus
ALL *things bright and beautiful,*
All creatures great and small,
All things wise and wonderful,
Evolved through a process involving combinations of amino acids.

EACH *little flower that opens,*
Each little bird that sings,
Their glowing colours were produced by pigmentation
Carried genetically via messenger DNA,
Their tiny wings are the product of centuries of evolution through Natural Selection.

THE *purple-headed mountain,*
The river running by,
Were formed by glacial movement
In the Pre-Cambrian era,
And the subterranean movement of magma.

OUR *stereoscopic vision*
is the product of our arboreal ancestors,
And the vocalisation process allows us to propagate the idea of a deity in the first place
Which is pretty incredible when you think about it.

AMEN

The last line of the first verse of the original version ends 'The Lord God made them all'. What does the changed last line imply about the Bishop of Durham's beliefs?

Find examples of similar changes.

Find other examples of parody and try some of your own.

12 Images

Why is a poem like a pop star?
They both need a good image!

If you were asked to describe Marilyn Monroe you would not be lost for words – there is a great deal you could say about this famous sex symbol. Many books have been written about her (and are still being written), and she is the subject of films, documentaries and magazine articles. Yet when Elton John and Bernie Taupin wrote a song about her, they did not overload it with too much descriptive detail but concentrated on a few striking *images* instead – the most vivid of these give the song its title, 'Candle in the Wind'. The image of a candle in the wind tells us a great deal about Marilyn's life and the kind of person she was. The more we think about it, the more it tells us. This is why poets make great use of imagery. It is more concise and vivid than a purely factual description could be.

Read or listen to the song, paying special attention to the way in which imagery is used.

CANDLE IN THE WIND

Goodbye Norma Jean
Though I never knew you at all
You had the grace to hold yourself
While those around you crawled.

They crawled out of the woodwork
And they whispered into your brain,
They set you on a treadmill,
And they made you change your name.

And it seems to me you lived your life
Like a candle in the wind
Never knowing who to cling to
When the rain set in.

Loneliness was tough,
The toughest role you ever played,
Hollywood created a superstar
And pain was the price you paid.

Even when you died
Oh the press still hounded you,
All the papers had to say
Was that Marilyn was found in the nude.

And I would have liked to have known you
But I was just a kid,
Your candle had burned out long before
Your legend ever did.

Goodbye Norma Jean
From the young man in the twenty-second row
Who sees you as something more than sexual,
More than just Marilyn Monroe.

Elton John and Bernie Taupin

123

A Closer Look

Notice that images are brought in in two ways:

- by using the words 'like' or 'as', for example '*Like* a candle in the wind'; this is called a *simile*;

- or more directly, for example, 'They set you on a treadmill' (the image of a treadmill – a mill worked by human power – shows how hard they made her work); this is called a *metaphor*.

You do not need to worry too much about these technical terms, what really matters is that you can respond to images, and explain how they add to the effectiveness of a poem. For example, you might write something like this:

'The press still hounded you' uses an image from hunting with a pack of hounds. It emphasises how cruelly the journalists pursued Marilyn – tracking her down like a hunted animal.

Try this for yourself by writing about the imagery in the whole song. Give particular attention to the main image 'candle in the wind' and show how it is linked to 'your candle burned out . . .'.

Study the following two poems in the same way, looking particularly for the imagery which is used to describe the girls in the poems:

SPLENDID GIRLS

Those splendid girls at the wheels of powerful cars,
Sheer mechanism setting off slender charms.
I glimpse daredevil smiles as they whip past.

What are they all eager for, driving so fast
That I see them only momentarily? They are
Wholly desirable for half a heart-beat.

They have such style, such red nails! They are so neat!
But though they appear to drive at a dangerous speed
They do not do anything at random, that's for sure.

So keep your shirt on, they are spoken for.
They are as bright and lively as advertisements
For cigarettes or petrol or soap.

But there is no danger, and there is no hope.
Those reckless smiles have been carefully painted.
They are that sort of doll.

Everything, but everything, is under control.

John Normanton

124

OLD MOVIES

How I loved those old movies
they would show in the Roxys
and Regals amongst all that
gilt plaster, or in the Bijou
flea-pits smelling of Jeyes.
The men sleek haired and suited,
with white cuffs and big trilbies,
the girls all pushovers,
wide-eyed with lashes
like venus fly traps and their
clouds of blonde candyfloss
for hair. Oh those bosoms, hips
and those long long legs
I never saw in daylight!
And their apartments,
vast as temples,
full of unusued furniture,
the sideboards bending with booze,
and all those acres of bed!
She, in attendance, wearing
diaphanous, but never quite
diaphanous enough, nightwear.
And their lives!
Where the baddies only,
if not always, stopped one,
and they loved and loved
and never ended up married.
Every time I get a whiff
of that disinfectant
I feel nostalgic.

John Cotton

Robert Cottingham, *Roxy*, 1972

GO, LOVELY ROSE

Go, lovely rose,
Tell her, that wastes her time and me,
That now she knows,
When I resemble her to thee,
How sweet and fair she seems to be.

Tell her that's young
And shuns to have her graces spied,
That hadst thou sprung
In deserts, where no men abide,
Thou must have uncommended died.

Small is the worth
Of beauty from the light retired;
Bid her come forth,
Suffer herself to be desired,
And not blush so to be admired.

Then die! that she
The common fate of all things rare
May read in thee:
How small a part of time they share
That are so wondrous sweet and fair!

Edmund Waller

THE ROSE

Some say love it is a river
That drowns the tender reed.
Some say love it is a razor
That leaves your soul to bleed.
Some say love it is a hunger
An endless aching need
I say love it is a flower
And you say it's only seed.

It's the heart afraid of breaking
That never learns to dance.
It's the dream afraid of waking
That never takes a chance.
It's the one who won't be taken
Who cannot seem to give
And the soul afraid of dying
That never learns to live.

When the night has been too lonely
And the road has been too long
And you think that love is only
For the lucky and the strong
Just remember in the winter
Far beneath the bitter snow
Lies the seed that with the sun's love
In the spring becomes the rose.

Amanda McBroom

(Sung by Elaine Paige in the film *The Rose*)

This poem and this song both use a rose as an image for love. Examine the different ways this image has been developed.

FAREWELL POEM

(Second of two to a girl of Yang-chou)

Passion too deep seems like none.
While we drink, nothing shows but the smile which will not come.
The wax candles feel, suffer at partings:
Their tears drip for us till the sky brightens.

Tu Mu

35 FEET DEEP IN THE WET LANGUAGE

35 feet deep in the wet language
my love lies buried, delectable;
my love lies blue without breathing
35 feet deep in the wet language.

O to be air
and around her!
But I'm not air and she's not mine.
And so I pour

yet more words into the hole,
lovingly, lovingly;
35 feet, 50 feet, 100 feet, 1000 feet
the words rise over her, all begging her to breathe.

But how can she breathe, thus all cemented up?
Forgive me my pleas without end, forgive me these 92 more words, my love . . .

John O Thompson

These two poems are built around a single, striking image. Explain why the image in each poem is so unusual. '35 feet deep in the wet language' is particularly striking. Explain in your own words what the poet is trying to say.

Try writing a short poem of your own around a single striking image.

ODE TO A WORM

Creature of the gloom . . .
Soft pink skin, corrugated into his
Soft, succulent body.
Blind, you grope in the light,
Wriggle, curl, you cannot see
Until the caverns of earth surround you,
You know each stone, each buried treasure,
Each fold of earth in your domain,
Oh muted subject to the underworld.
Repulsive worm.

Elasticated! Stretched and tugged
Beyond endurance – yet still you exert
Cruel sharp beak; it isn't fair.
You are a take-away.
Does your life spin before you?
Don't you wish you had something else?
Instead, you are turned away,
Poor worm!

Alison Rostron, aged 14

SPIDER

Slow
As a limping cow
Or a mighty bull
With its legs split in two,
A great black spider comes out of the earth,
And climbs up the wall,
Then painfully sets his back against the trees,
Throws out his threads for the wind to carry,
Weaves a web that reaches the sky
And spreads his net across the blue . . .

Jean-Joseph Rabearivelo

THE CAT

Pleasures that I most enviously sense,
  Pass in long ripples down her flanks and stir
  The plume that is her tail. She deigns to purr
And take caresses. But her paws would tense
To flashing weapons at the least offence.
  Humbly I bend to stroke her silken fur,
  I am content to be a slave to her
I am enchanted by her insolence.

Not one of all the women I have known
  Has been so beautiful, or proud, or wise
  As this Angora with her amber eyes.
She makes her chosen cushion seem a throne,
  And wears the same voluptuous, slow smile
  She wore when she was worshipped on the Nile.

W Adolphe Roberts

THE KITTEN

Warm and purring like a new car's engine,
Kitten in my lap,
Her head, a gingery apple under my hand.
She yawns,
Her teeth are sharp and pointed,
Her tongue, pinkish-red and sandpaper-rough.

She rolls over onto her stomach,
Her fluffy tigerish chops rubbing my leg.
A sound!
Her ears stand up, pointed, thin and delicate.
She miaows expressively
As if to say 'What is it, what do you want?'
She looks around
With her big mustard-yellow black slit-centred eyes
And settles down on my lap again
Her soft downy chest like ducks' feathers
Rubbing on my legs.

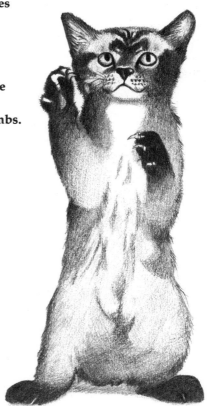

She presses her tiny cotton wool-ball paws into me
Her sharp claws pierce like pins
As she pushes herself off my knee with her fragile limbs.
She mischievously leaps up the curtains
And her little bell tinkles.
Her instincts tell her it's time for a drink.
She laps the milk like a dainty old lady,
Then runs into the garden.

It's cold outside!
Her fur puffs out like a mane,
She shudders
And slinks back sheepishly
To my warm lap.

Anne Middleton, aged 15

How do the images in these four poems help to describe the animals more vividly?
Write your own animal poem using imagery to enhance the description.

The poem 'Very Like a Whale' by Ogden Nash takes a humorous look at the way in which poets use (or over-use!) simile and metaphor.

VERY LIKE A WHALE

One thing that literature would be greatly better for

Would be a more restricted employment by authors of simile and metaphor.

Authors of all races, be they Greeks, Romans, Teutons, or Celts,

Can't seem just to say that anything is the thing it is but have to go out of their way to say that it is like something else.

What does it mean we are told

That the Assyrian came down like a wolf on the fold?

In the first place, George Gordon Byron had had enough experience

To know that it probably wasn't just one Assyrian, it was a lot of Assyrians.

However, as too many arguments are apt to induce apoplexy and thus hinder longevity,

We'll let it pass as one Assyrian for the sake of brevity.

Now then, this particular Assyrian, the one whose cohorts were gleaming in purple and gold,

Just what does the poet mean when he says he came down like a wolf on the fold?

In heaven and earth more than is dreamed of in our philosophy there are a great many things,

But I don't imagine that among them there is a wolf with purple and gold cohorts or purple and gold anythings.

No, no, Lord Byron, before I'll believe that this Assyrian was actually like a wolf I must have some kind of proof;

Did he run on all fours and did he have a hairy tail and a big red mouth and bit white teeth and did he say Woof woof?

Frankly I think it very unlikely, and all you were entitled to say, at the most,

Was that the Assyrian cohorts came down like a lot of Assyrian cohorts about to destroy the Hebrew host.

130

But that wasn't fancy enough for Lord Byron, oh dear me
no, he had to invent a lot of figures of speech and then
interpolate them,
With the result that whenever you mention Old Testament
soldiers to people they say Oh yes, they're the ones
that a lot of wolves dressed up in gold and purple ate
them.
That's the kind of thing that's being done all the time by
poets, from Homer to Tennyson;
They're always comparing ladies to lilies and veal to
venison,
And they always say things like that the snow is a white
blanket after a winter storm.
Oh it is, is it, all right then, you sleep under a six-inch
blanket of snow and I'll sleep under a half-inch blanket
of unpoetical blanket material and we'll see which one
keeps warm.
And after that maybe you'll begin to comprehend dimly
What I mean by too much metaphor and simile.

Ogden Nash

Ogden Nash gives this example of a simile: 'The Assyrian came down like a wolf on the fold'. How do we know that this is a simile? What is this simile meant to emphasise about the Assyrian attack? Do you think this is an effective simile? What are Ogden Nash's criticisms of it?

Later in the poem he makes fun of an often-used metaphor. What is it? What does he say about it? Do you agree with him?

Over to You

Write an essay about one of the poems in this chapter with special reference to the use of imagery. These suggestions may be used as a guide:

- Begin with a short paragraph saying simply and clearly what the poem is about.

- Write about the imagery in the poem – draw on any notes you made while working through the chapter.

- Write about the use of rhyme, rhythm and any other interesting features of the poem.

- End with your personal response – your thoughts and feelings about the poem and the way it was written.

Diversions

This little poem is making an important statement about poetry today, but because it is written as a series of images you might mistake it for a nature poem at first reading. See if you can work out what the poem is saying (clue: think about what the birds and frogs represent). You will find the answer on page 166.

POETRY TODAY

The sun is eclipsed; and one by one
The birds stop singing –
Folded their wings:

But I never heard
That the frogs stopped croaking.

John Heath-Stubbs

13 Pop Poetry

Poets get their poems in the Top 20.

Adrian Henri

Because poets work at the frontiers of language, and are often trying to put into words thoughts and feelings for which there are no words, their work can become so complex that only a privileged few can understand it. The same can be said of much modern 'classical' music and art. This is one reason why the 'pop' movement began in the 1950s – 'pop', of course, being short for 'popular'. Pop music has been the biggest success, but there was also a 'pop art' movement, and an even lesser-known one called 'pop poetry'.

These were the principles of pop art as written down by Richard Hamilton in 1957:

> *Pop should be:*
> *Popular (designed for a mass audience)*
> *Transient (short-term solution)*
> *Expendable (easily forgotten)*
> *Low-cost*
> *Mass-produced*
> *Young (aimed at youth)*
> *Witty*
> *Sexy*
> *Gimmicky*
> *Glamorous*
> *Big business . . .*

Think about and discuss these principles and then see how they apply to the examples of pop art and poetry in this chapter.

TONIGHT AT NOON

Tonight at noon
Supermarkets will advertise 3d EXTRA on everything
Tonight at noon
Children from happy families will be sent to live in a home
Elephants will tell each other human jokes
America will declare peace on Russia
World War I generals will sell poppies in the streets on November 11th
The first daffodils of autumn will appear
When the leaves fall upwards to the trees

Tonight at noon
Pigeons will hunt cats through city backyards
Hitler will tell us to fight on the beaches and on the landing fields
A tunnel full of water will be built under Liverpool
Pigs will be sighted flying in formation over Woolton
and Nelson will not only get his eye back but his arm as well
White Americans will demonstrate for equal rights
in front of the Black House
and the Monster has just created Dr Frankenstein

Girls in bikinis are moonbathing
Folksongs are being sung by real folk
Artgalleries are closed to people over 21
Poets get their poems in the Top 20.
Politicians are elected to insane asylums
There's jobs for everyone and nobody wants them
In back alleys everywhere teenage lovers are kissing
in broad daylight
In forgotten graveyards everywhere the dead will quietly
bury the living
and
You will tell me you love me
Tonight at noon

Adrian Henri

134

Eduardo Paolozzi, *I Was a Rich Man's Plaything*, 1947

135

From 'SUMMER WITH MONIKA': 39

monika the teathings are taking over!
the cups are as big as bubble cars
they throttle round the room
tinopeners skate on the greasy plates
by the light of the silvery moon
the biscuits are having a knees-up
they're necking in our breadbin
that's jazz you hear from the saltcellars
but they don't let non members in
the egg spoon's had our eggs for breakfast
the sauce bottle's asleep in our bed
i overheard the knives and forks
'it won't be long' they said
'it won't be long' they said

Roger McGough

Richard Hamilton, *Just what is it that makes today's homes so different, so appealing?*, 1956

136

WHERE ARE YOU NOW SUPERMAN?

The serials are all wound up now,
Put away in small black boxes
For a decade or so. Superman's asleep
In the sixpenny childhood seats,
Batman and Robin are elsewhere
And can't see the Batsign thrown out
By kids with toffee-smeared mouths.
Captain Marvel's SHAZAM! echoes round the auditorium,
But the magicians don't hear him,
Must all be dead . . .
The Purple Monster who came down from the Purple Planet
Disguised as a man, is wandering aimlessly about the streets
With no way of getting back.
Sir Galahad's been strangled by the Incredible Living Trees,
Zorro killed by his own sword.
Blackhawk's buried his companions
In the disused hangars of innocence
And Flash Gordon likewise wanders lonely,
Weeping over the girl he loved 7 Universes ago.

We killed them all simply because we grew up;
We made them possible with our uneducated minds
And with our pocket money
And the sixpences we received
For pretending to be Good.
We think we are too old to cheer and boo now,
But let's not kid ourselves,
We still cheer and boo
But do it quietly or at General Elections
Where it's still possible to find a goodie
Now and then.

Clark Kent (alias Superman)
Committed suicide because he failed to find new roles.
The bullets that bounced off him on the screen
Wormed their way in in Real Life.
But who cared for real life?
We had our own world, our own celluloid imaginations
And now we have a different world,
One that's a little more cynical
And we believe, a little more real.

Our batsignals now questions flung into space
To attract the attention of passing solutions . . .

Brian Patten

137

A recent 'pop poem'?

Busy Day

Pop in
pop out
pop over the road
pop out for a walk
pop in for a talk
pop down to the shop
can't stop
got to pop

got to pop?

pop where?
pop what?

well
I've got to
pop round
pop up
pop in to town
pop out and see
pop in for tea
pop down to the shop
can't stop
got to pop

got to pop?

pop where?
pop what?

well
I've got to
pop in
pop out
pop over the road
pop out for a walk
pop in for a talk . . . .

Michael
Rosen

138

Here are some examples of 'Beat Poetry' – the American equivalent of 'pop poetry':

CONSTANTLY risking absurdity
                              and death
                whenever he performs
                                    above the heads
                                            of his audience
            the poet like an acrobat
                    climbs on rime
                            to a high wire of his own making
    and balancing on eyebeams
                            above a sea of faces
            paces his way
                        to the other side of day
        performing entrechats
                        and sleight-of-foot tricks
        and other high theatrics
                        and all without mistaking
            any thing
                    for what it may not be

    For he's the super realist
                        who must perforce perceive
            taut truth
                    before the taking of each stance or step
    in his supposed advance
                        toward that still higher perch
    where Beauty stands and waits
                        with gravity
                            to start her death-defying
                                        leap
And he
            a little charleychaplin man
                        who may or may not catch
            her fair eternal form
                        spreadeagled in the empty air
        of existence.

                                        Lawrence Ferlinghetti

139

FOND FAREWELL TO THE CHICAGO REVIEW

All these demands for my voice, my voice
Wrapped up in a ball rolled under the bureau

Retrieved with the help of the vacuum-cleaner
It just won't work any more

I whack it with a hammer & all it says is

>Plato
>Plautus
>Pliny
>Plotinus
>Plutarch

>before it falls apart

In the garbagecan the pieces hum vague fitful music in the
dark.

From now on it's the Harpo Marx routine for me:
Creating wordless havoc in pursuit of blondes.

Philip Whalen

There is, of course, another kind of pop poetry – the lyrics to pop songs. Some of these are interesting enough to stand on their own without music. Here is one example. Can you think of any others?

JUNGLELAND

The Rangers had a homecoming in Harlem late last night
And the Magic Rat drove his sleek machine over the Jersey state line
Barefoot girl sitting on the hood of a Dodge
Drinking warm beer in the soft summer rain
The Rat pulls into town, rolls up his pants, together they take a stab at romance
And disappear down Flamingo Lane.

Well the Maximum Lawmen run down Flamingo chasing the Rat and the barefoot girl
And the kids round here look just like shadows, always quiet, holding hands
From the churches to the jails, tonight all is silence in the world,
As we take our stand, down in Jungleland.

The midnight gang's assembled and picked a rendezvous for the night
They'll meet 'neath that giant Exxon sign that brings this fair city light
Man there's an opera out on the turnpike, there's a ballet being fought in the alley
Until the local cops, Cherry Tops, rips this holy night
The streets alive as secret debts are paid, contacts made they vanish unseen
Kids flash guitars just like switch-blades, hustling for the record machine
The hungry and the hunted explode into rock and roll bands
That face off against each other out in the street, down in Jungleland.

In the parking lot the visionaries dress in the latest rage,
Inside the backstreet girls are dancing to the records that the D.J. plays
Lonely-hearted lovers struggle in dark corners, desperate as the night moves on
Just one look, and a whisper, and they're gone.

Beneath a city, two hearts beat, soul engines running through a night so tender
In a bedroom locked in whispers of soft refusal and then surrender
In the tunnels uptown the Rat's own dream guns him down
As shots echo down them hallways in the night
No one watches as the ambulance pulls away, or as the girl shuts out the bedroom light.

Outside the street's on fire in a red death waltz, between what's flesh and what's fantasy,
And the poets down here don't write nothing at all, they just stand back and let it all be,
And in the quick of the night they reach for their moment and try to make an honest stand,
But they wind up wounded not even dead tonight in Jungleland.

Bruce Springsteen

141

Talking Points

How many of Richard Hamilton's principles (see page 133) apply to pop music?

How many apply to the examples of pop art? Are there any that may have applied at the time, but have since been contradicted?

How many apply to the pop poems in this chapter? Which principles seem to go against the true nature of poetry?

Over to You

The pop poetry movement has died out, which is a pity, because poetry has a great deal to offer and can be very enjoyable. What is needed is a new generation of poets who can write poetry with a wide appeal – popular poetry. Perhaps some of them are reading these words at this moment – if so, why not begin with a list of principles which you think would make poetry popular, and then try to write some poems based on those principles. Who knows, in a few years time there may be poetry charts, a poetry number one, and *you* might be the first poetry millionaire!

Diversions

The poem opposite is a 'cut-up' poem. It was made by cutting up a copy of Wordsworth's poem 'Daffodils' and a Dutch motor-car leaflet and combining the pieces. It would be interesting to read through the poem and try to pick out which is which. If you wished, you could find a copy of Wordsworth's 'Daffodils' to help you. Try your own 'cut-up' poems. For example, you could do a poetry version of the 'montage' pictures on pages 135 and 136 by cutting and mixing advertisements, teenage magazines, sweet wrappers, brand labels, etc.

THE NEW, FAST, AUTOMATIC DAFFODILS

(New variation on Wordsworth's 'Daffodils')

I wandered lonely as
THE NEW, FAST DAFFODIL
   FULLY AUTOMATIC
that floats on high o'er vales and hills
The Daffodil is generously dimensioned to accommo-
   date four adult passengers
10,000 saw I at a glance
Nodding their new anatomically shaped heads in
   sprightly dance
Beside the lake beneath the trees
    in three bright modern colours
red, blue and pigskin
The Daffodil de luxe is equipped with a host of useful
   accessories
including windscreen wiper and washer with joint
   control
A Daffodil doubles the enjoyment of touring at home
   or abroad

in vacant or in pensive mood
SPECIFICATION:
    Overall width   1·44m (57″)
    Overall height   1·38m (54·3″)
    Max. speed   105 km/hr (65 m.p.h.)
     (also cruising speed)

DAFFODIL
   RELIABLE – ECONOMICAL
DAFFODIL
   THE BLISS OF SOLITUDE
DAFFODIL
   The Variomatic Inward Eye
Travelling by Daffodil you can relax and enjoy every
   mile of the journey.

Adrian Henri

14 Experimental Poetry

Poetry is a search for the inexplicable.

Wallace Stevens

Science is changing the world, and if poetry is to help us understand this rapidly changing world, it too must change. While scientists are seeking to push back the frontiers of knowledge, poets are trying to extend their range of expression – trying to make language express more and express it in different ways. To do this, they need to experiment. Many of these experiments will lead nowhere, but some, like Walt Whitman's free verse a hundred years ago, will point the way to the future. Here are some examples of experiments with poetry – some of them so extreme that you may be forgiven for wondering how they can be called poetry at all. You will therefore find much in this chapter that is strange and new – and exciting. The important thing is to keep an open mind and let each poem communicate to you in its own way.

MIRROR

When you look
into a mirror
it is not
yourself you see,
but a kind
of apish error
posed in fearful
symmetry.

kool uoy nehW
rorrim a otni
ton si ti
‚ees uoy flesruoy
dnik a tub
rorre hsipa fo
lufraef ni desop
.yrtemmys

John Updike

144

FORSYTHIA

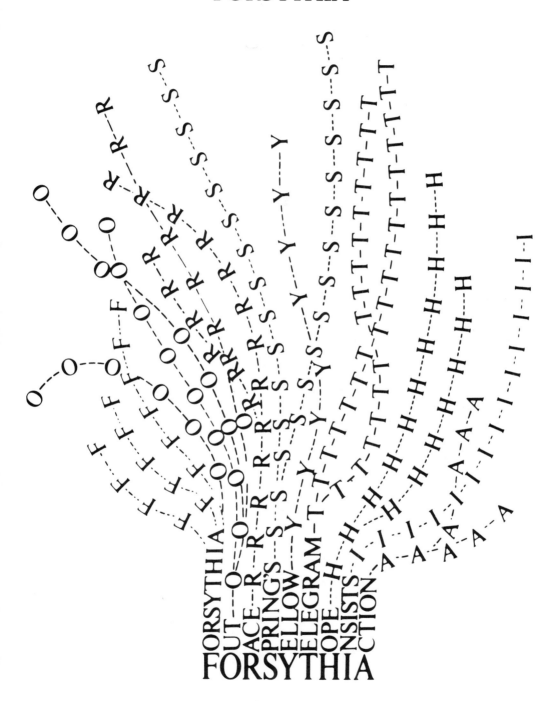

FORSYTHIA

Mary Ellen Solt

MOONSHOT SONNET

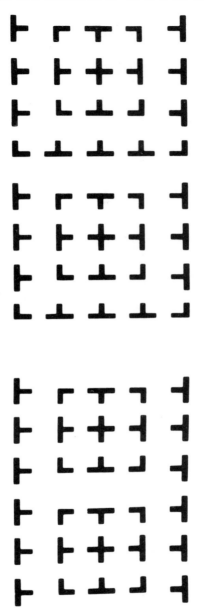

Mary Ellen Solt

Notes on the Poem:
'Moonshot Sonnet' (1964). The poem was found on the moon photos in the *New York Times*. When the scientists' symbols were simply copied, there were fourteen 'lines' with five 'accents'. Design: Mary Ellen Solt. Drawings: Timothy Mayer.

THE FUTURE

The Future does not look like this . . .

The Future looks more like this . . .

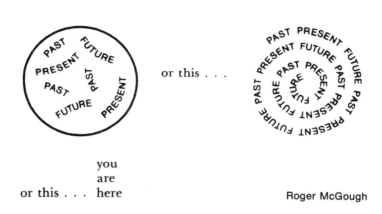

or this . . .

Roger McGough

FROM RAGS TO RICHES

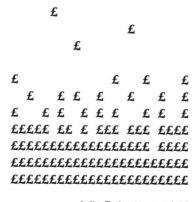

Julie Roberts, aged 15

KITE

My son
had a kite
which shimmered like
fish scales in the sun
as it lay dead on the ground.
Then it trembled to life with the breath
of swinging wind and sang far, far away
in clear air till it hung its wings on the sky.
He bit hard at the straining line like a played fish
drawn to the tune that the kite dreamed
until it became a frenzied cry,
a dance in him,
with its tail
snaking,
body
flickering,
wire
vibrant.
But suddenly
the taut string

SNAPPED

and with
the life-cord

C
U
T

it hesitated,
out
of
tune,
and dived,
trapped
by
the
earth.

David Watkin Price

SNAKE GLIDES

Snake glides
through grass
over
pebbles
forked tongue
working
never
speaking
but its
body
whispers
listen

Keith Bosley

148

AN ELIZABETHAN EXPERIMENTAL POEM

Her Majestie, for Many Parts in her most Noble and Vertuous Nature to be found, resembleth to the Spire.

(Ye must begin beneath, according to the nature of the Device)

Skie
Azured
In the
Assur'de

And better
and richer
much greater

Crown and empir
After an hier
For to aspire
Like flame of fire
In form of Spire

To mount on hie
Con-ti-nu-al-ly
With travel and teen.
Most gracious Queen
Ye have made a vow
Shews us plainly how
Not fained but true
To everyman's vew
Shining cleere in you
Of so bright an hewe
Even thus vertewe

Vanish out of sight
Till his fine top be quite
To taper in the ayre
Endevours soft and faire,
By his kindly nature,
Of tall comely stature
Like as this faire figure

Anon

COMMON SENSE

An agricultural labourer, who has
A wife and four children, receives 20s a week.
$\frac{3}{4}$ buys food, and the members of the family
Have three meals a day.
How much is that per person per meal?
> –*From Pitman's Common Sense Arithmetic, 1917*

A gardener, paid 24s a week, is
Fined 1/3 if he comes to work late.
At the end of 26 weeks, he receives
£30.5.3. How
Often was he late?
> –*From Pitman's Common Sense Arithmetic, 1917*

A milk dealer buys milk at 3d a quart. He
Dilutes it with 3% water and sells
124 gallons of the mixture at
4d per quart. How much of his profit is made by
Adulterating the milk?
> –*From Pitman's Common Sense Arithmetic, 1917*

The table printed below gives the number
Of paupers in the United Kingdom, and
The total cost of poor relief.
Find the average number
Of paupers per ten thousand people.
    – From Pitman's Common Sense Arithmetic, 1917

An army had to march to the relief of
A besieged town, 500 miles away, which
Had telegraphed that it could hold out for 18 days.
The army made forced marches at the rate of 18
Miles a day. Would it be there in time?
    – From Pitman's Common Sense Arithmetic, 1917

Out of an army of 28,000 men,
15% were
Killed, 25% were
Wounded. Calculate
How many men there were left to fight.
    – From Pitman's Common Sense Arithmetic, 1917

These sums are offered to
That host of young people in our Elementary Schools, who
Are so ardently desirous of setting
Foot upon the first rung of the
Educational ladder . . .
    – From Pitman's Common Sense Arithmetic, 1917

Alan Brownjohn

A Closer Look

This is what Alan Brownjohn says about 'Common Sense':

> *I took six of the sums, re-arranged them just a little, and set them out in verses of poetry to make a satirical poem about the world of 1917 (the last verse is taken from the introduction to the book). This is what is called, I suppose, a 'found' poem rather than a written one.*

In your opinion, can words taken from an arithmetic textbook with few changes be called poetry?

10

v. trendy things to do
1960s style

- If you were a girl, wiggle like Marilyn, if you weren't, swagger like James Dean

- Read magazines devoted to film stars

- Chew gum

- Go to the flicks (or a drive-in movie if you were a Yank)

- Tune into the wireless (as a radio was then known before Mike Smith was invented!)

- Go 'tonning' – or riding with your boyfriend on his speedy bike

- Bopping and rocking at dance-halls

- Be a 'beatnik' (they were into jazz, had v. alternative views and wore scruffy dark clothes so The Steve would have made a good one . . .)

- Watch early versions of Top of the Pops, like 'Ready Steady Go' and 'Juke Box Jury' on TV

- Mime along to your fave discs on your dansette – a cute, compact record-player

Poem 'found' by Sarah Cottam, aged 14, in *Jackie*

How many 'poems' of this kind can you find? Mount the best one on file paper and write about your reasons for choosing it.

PROSE POEM TOWARDS A DEFINITION OF ITSELF

When in public poetry should take off its clothes and wave to the nearest person in sight; It should be seen in the company of thieves and lovers rather than that of journalists and publishers. On sighting mathematicians it should unhook the algebra from their minds and replace it with poetry; on sighting poets it shoulld unhook poetry from the minds and replace it with algebra: it should touch those people who despise being touched, it should fall in love with children and woo them with fairytales; it should wait on the landing for two years for its mates to come home then go outside and find them all dead.

When the electricity fails it should wear dark glasses and pretend to be blind. It should guide those who are safe into the middle of busy roads and leave them there. It should scatter woodworm into the bedrooms of all peg-legged men, not being afraid to hurt the innocent; It should shout EVIL! EVIL! EVIL! from the roofs of stock exchanges. It should not pretend to be a clerk or librarian. It is the eventual sameness of contradictions. It should never weep unless it is alone, and then only after it has covered the mirrors and sealed up the cracks. Poetry is the astronaut stepping for the first time into liquid space; it is the brilliant fish chattering in the deep pool; the bomb exploding for no particular reason over the deserted villages; the unicorn dying on the edge of the new industrial estates; the albatross laughing as at last it enters the wedding feast.

Poetry should seek out pale and lyrical couples and wander with them into stables, neglected bedrooms, engineless cars, unsafe forests, for A Final Good Time. It should enter burning factories too late to save anybody. It should pay no attention to its name.

Poetry should seen to be lying by the side of road accidents, hissing from unlit gas-rings. It should scrawl the nymph's secret on her teacher's blackboard, offer her a worm saying: Inside this is a tiny apple. At dawn it should leave the bedroom and catch the first bus home to its wife. At dusk it should chat up a girl nobody wants. It should be seen standing on the ledge of a skyscraper, on a bridge with a brick tied around its heart. Poetry is the monster hiding in a child's dark room. It is the scar on a beautiful person's face. It is the last blade of grass being picked from the city park.

Brian Patten

Is this poetry? Is the term 'prose poem' a contradiction?

Discuss Brian Patten's ideas about the nature of poetry.

Talking Points

Is there anything that has been expressed in these poems that could not be expressed in any other way?

Have any of the poems made you see something in a new light? What was it?

Do you think the examples in this chapter are really poetry? Refer back to Chapter 2, 'What is Poetry?', to help you decide. Why not organise a class debate on the subject?

Over to You

Write a poem, a piece of prose, or even a 'prose poem' stating your opinions about the nature of poetry.

Write some experimental poems based on the examples in this chapter. Be daring – take risks! One of the exciting things about poetry is that there are no rules except those you choose for yourself. Here are some suggestions to help you:

- Look again at 'Forsythia' on page 145, and write similar poems about trees and flowers.

- How do you see your future? Write a diagram poem similar to Roger McGough's poem 'The Future' on page 147.

- What is the most boring textbook in use in your school? Do what Alan Brownjohn did in 'Common Sense' on pages 150 and 151, and transform part of it into a poem!

Diversions

This is another type of experimental poem – a code poem. Study it carefully and then work out its meaning by using the key on page 156. Discuss your reaction to it, and then try writing your own code poem using the same symbols.

MARRIAGE

Mary Ellen Solt

Marriage: Key to the code

MARRIAGE

A code poem derived from the universal language of signs and symbols used from primitive times to the present day:

the alphabet
astrology astronomy botany
chemistry commerce engineering
mathematics medicine
meteorology music physics
punctuation runes zoology &c.

◆ *dot: secrecy origin of all signs*
◇ *diamond female anatomical symbol*
♡ *heart*
♡ *composite symbol*
✡ *perfect marriage*
✡ *composite symbol*
L *length (terrestrial) lambert: unit of brightness right angle: meeting of the celestial (vertical) and the terrestrial (horizontal)*
O *oxygen ocean blood type of husband and wife October (unofficial): husband's birth month*
V *potential energy velocity volume*
E *earth excellent*
LEO *husband's name*

I Pairings

- ☿ *sun (old oriental symbol) source of all life*
- ⦶ *active male element saltpeter*
- ⊖ *passive female element earth (with equator) salt element: water*
- ♂ *male male flower*
- ♀ *female female flower planet Venus mirror of Venus*
- ▽ *male element: water*
- △ *female wisdom godhead element: fire*
- □ *male*
- ○ *female new moon unborn child God eternity element: fire*
- 𝄞 *treble clef*
- 𝄢 *bass clef*
- ⊙ *sun open eye of God element: air*
- ⊕ *earth creation: male plus female sun cross element: earth*
- =○= *equivalent*
- △ *finite difference*
- 𝅝 *whole note*
- XX *double strength*
- m+f=f+m *commutative law*
- M—F *male implies female*
- F—M *female implies male*

II Conjugations

- ⚳ *Ceres: goddess of earth's fertility*
- ♡ *love*
- © *copyright*
- ⇔ *reversible reaction*
- F° *degrees of heat warmth*
- 𝄐 *hold*
- ♮ *natural*
- 𝄇 *repeat*
- V *up-bow*
- Λ *down-bow*
- A *first class vessel*
- X *kiss the unknown takes (chess)*
- ∝ *varies as*
- → *give*
- ℞ *take*
- *X* *reactance*
- *R* *resistance*
- ☾ *the moon's phases*
- ▷— *man & woman united: procreation*
- ⅄ *pregnant woman*
- ☆ *the five senses happy homecoming*

III Family

- ⋇ *family: man with wife and children*
- S *Solt school sulfur combustible elements*
- s *plural stem sire son sister series*
- 's *contraction: us is has possessive*
- ᚾ *(rune: nied) necessity thraldom*
- ᛘ *man*
- ⅄ *woman*
- ▷∘ *woman bears child*
- ⊙ *moment of birth: awakening of inner life in body*
- ♎ *Libra: astrological sign of father*
- ♋ *Cancer: astrological sign of mother*
- ♊ *Gemini: astrological sign of daughter*
- ♒ *Aquarius: astrological sign of daughter*
- ♃ *planet Jupiter: name of family cat*
- Ms. *female of undefined status: name of family dog*
- % *in care of*
- ; *related and continuing*
- ∩ *intersection: shared in common*
- ⊠ *simple activity*
- ♪ *appoggiatura: grace note*
- ᚼ *unity*

IV Home

- ⚷ *key*
- ⌂ *house*
- ᚹ *(rune: wynn) comfort*
- ▣ *orderliness*
- ✹ *disorder*
- ᚺ *chair*
- ⚲ *frying pan*
- ψ *fork*
- ⊹ *olive oil*
- ⚶ *vinegar*
- ⊞ *water*
- ⊹ *borax*
- ✝ *wood*
- ⚴ *glass*
- ♃ *lime*
- ♄ *tree*
- $ *money*
- ℅ *account*
- % *mortgage*
- ᛟ *(rune: ogal) possession*
- ⌘ *to exorcise evil spirits*

15 Putting it Together

A poem is only a little word machine.

Miroslav Holub

Much of this book has been concerned with taking these 'word machines' to pieces to find out how they work. But the separate parts of a poem do not work in isolation: they make their full impact together. We must therefore reassemble the machines – in other words, bring together everything covered in previous chapters to appreciate poetry to the full. The guides in this chapter will help you to do this and to apply what you have learned to a wide range of approaches to poetry.

Studying a Poem

The following three-point guide can be used as the basis of an essay plan, and could be particularly helpful when writing about 'unprepared' poems. However, it is very important that you use it flexibly. Whatever you do, do not tailor what you say about a poem to fit the guide – it should be the other way around – alter and adapt it to suit the poem.

1 What is the poet saying?

Read the poem carefully a number of times until you are sure you understand it. Do not forget to read the title, as this may help you to understand the poem (see 'Diversions' page 79). Begin your discussion or writing with a clear account of what the poem is about.

2 How does he or she say it?

Comment on the following, as appropriate:

- Line layout and repetition (see pages 11–12, 32–44 and 70–80)
- Rhyme and rhythm (see pages 45–59 and 60–9)
- Use of language (see pages 81–104)
- Feeling (see pages 105–114)
- Imagery (see pages 122–32)

Note: This checklist is only a starting point. There are many other ways in which a poet can communicate to you. Try to be sensitive to the poem – let it communicate to you, and then try to explain how it has done this.

3 Your personal response

What are your thoughts and feelings about the subject of the poem? What interested you about it? Do you agree with the poet's point of view? Does the poem echo your own feelings and concerns?

Which of the features listed under point 2 were most successful in communicating to you (for example, an image which triggered your imagination, a rhyme which stressed a point, a thought-provoking play on words)?

What did you most like or dislike about the poem?

Writing

Go back over some of the poems which you like best, and look at them again the light of what you have read in this book. Use the guide as a basis for discussion and writing.

Use the guide to study poems from other sources.

When you have used the guide several times, and are thoroughly familiar with it, try to study a poem without it.

Studying a Theme

A *theme* is a general idea which runs through a group of poems: 'To whom it may concern' (page 42), 'Kill the Children' (page 111) and 'Base Details' (page 120) have different subjects, but share the theme of 'war'.

Begin by building up a collection of poems which are linked by a theme. This book will provide a good starting point, or you could refer to one of the many anthologies that are arranged thematically.

There are many ways in which you could write about your selection of poems. Here are two suggestions:

Plan 1

Introduction   Say briefly why you chose the theme and why it interests you.

A survey of the poems   Arrange the poems in some sort of order and work through them writing about how they present the theme in different ways. Briefly compare their different viewpoints. Do not go into too much detail at this stage.

Two or three poems in detail   Write about these poems as explained on page 157–8. Relate what you say to the theme whenever possible, particularly when writing your response.

A personal view   Refer back to your introduction – How has the study of these poems changed or developed your views on the theme? What final thoughts on the theme are you left with?

Plan 2

Choose a key poem which contains a very full statement of the theme and write about it in detail as explained in 'Studying a Poem' on pages 157–8. Bring in other poems at appropriate points as you go along. End with a personal view as described above. Note that this will need very careful planning and redrafting (see pages 162–3).

Writing

Try out one of these plans by going back over the book and finding all the poems on one of these themes:

childhood	money	war	characters
growing up	leisure	the media	animals.

You may also be able to think of other themes to link groups of poems.

Study of a Poet

When writing about a poet there are two things in particular to bear in mind: *theme* and *style*.

Theme

A poet may write about many different subjects, but these will be linked by a small number of themes. For example, a glance at Robert Frost's poems would reveal titles such as 'Mowing', 'After Apple Picking' and 'Birches', and you would soon realise that these different subjects are linked by the theme of 'country life'. Once you have identified a poet's main theme, or themes, you can write about them in the ways suggested on pages 158-9.

Style

A wide range of poetic techniques has been described in this book, but few poets make use of them all. They use combinations of these techniques in a way that is unique to them. Some poets, like D H Lawrence, prefer to use free verse, while others, like Edward Lucie-Smith, like to use rhyme and rhythm. Roger McGough is noted for his skilful wordplay and Mary Ellen Solt for her experimental poems. In fact, it is often possible to tell who wrote a poem simply by its style. This is particularly true of great poets whose styles are highly individual.

Suggested essay plan

Introduction   This could include a few words about why you chose that particular poet and/or some *brief* background information about the poet's life, etc.

Themes   Group the poems according to theme. For example, you might find four poems about 'country life', three about 'time' and four about 'religion'. It is likely that there will be a few poems left over that do not seem to fit in anywhere; these could be looked at in other ways (see below) or left out altogether.

Write about each theme in turn, working through the poems in each group and showing how they present the theme in different ways.

Style   Ask yourself: what is the most noticeable feature of this poet's work? ('Studying a poem' on pages 157-8 will remind you what to look for.) You may notice, for example, that the poet uses a great deal of vivid imagery. Write about this feature, explaining how it is used in a number of poems (turn back and revise the appropriate chapter, if necessary). Continue by writing about other features of the poet's work in the same way.

Two or three poems in detail   (Include or omit this section depending on the required length of the project.) Write in detail about two or three poems, remembering to show how the poems deal with the poet's main themes, and reflect his or her style.

Conclusion   This should include your personal response: what thoughts and feelings are you left with? What do you particularly admire/appreciate about this poet's work?

Writing

Which of the poets represented in this book did you particularly enjoy? Find several other poems by the same poet, in this book and other books and anthologies, and write about him or her as suggested on page 160.

Write an introduction to an edition of a poet's work. In many ways, this will be similar to what you have written for the previous question, but bear in mind the purpose of the introduction, and the intended audience. Read some real examples for inspiration.

Your response to poetry can take many other forms. Those you choose will depend on your own interests and abilities as well as the requirements of examination board syllabuses. In most cases a variety of work is best:

- Copy out a poem which deals with an issue which concerns you and write an 'answer' to it, agreeing or disagreeing with the poet in prose or verse.

- Rewrite a poem from a different point of view. For example, write about the granny in 'Rocking Gran Blues' (page 66) from the point of view of the teenagers in the disco.

- Copy out a poem and add more verses to it.

- Retell a poem as a prose story, making up events that lead into it and follow on from it.

- Take a scene from a novel you are reading and turn it into a poem.

- Find poems and song lyrics which go together, such as '19' and the poems about Vietnam in Chapter 4, and write about them.

- In small groups, prepare a poem for reading aloud, then develop it further into role play or drama.

- Make an extended study of a particular aspect of poetry – imagery, for example. Use the appropriate chapter in this book as a guide.

- Make a study of a particular poetic form – for example, free verse, sonnet, ballad, experimental poetry.

- Write a project entitled 'What is Poetry?'. Use material from this book as evidence.

- Write a booklet which presents a selection of poems to younger pupils. It could take the form of a coursebook similar to this one.

- Best of all, think of your own ideas for responses to a poem – the poem itself might suggest something to you.

Drafting

Few writers achieve what they want at their first attempt. This is particularly true of poets because they are trying to use words as effectively as possible. To achieve this they often have to write many versions, or *drafts*, of a poem, altering and improving until they are finally satisfied. Your own work would undoubtedly benefit from a more organised approach to drafting. The checklists below will help you.

Poetry

- If your poem is in free verse, could the layout of words and lines be altered to improve their effect?

- Could any words or phrases be repeated to give emphasis or create a pattern?

- If you have used rhyme, does it sound natural? Has it muddled the meaning? Are there any places where the rhythm sounds clumsy? Try changing the words – saying the same thing in a different way.

- Have you chosen exactly the right words? Why not check some of the key words of your poem with a thesaurus to see if there are any better alternatives?

- Have you used images which spark off the reader's imagination and help to portray your subject more vividly?

- Are you satisfied with the development of the ideas in your poem? Could they be expressed more clearly, thrown into clearer contrast, or pruned of waffle?

Other types of written work

- Have you written clearly? Is there enough detail? Is there anything that should be explained/described more fully? Have you taken care to use exactly the right word, and not just the first one that came into your head?

- Is the style and vocabulary appropriate for the intended audience?

- Is the work well planned, and divided into paragraphs if appropriate? Could the planning be improved by re-arrangement of certain sections? Could it be improved by adding more to it? For example, have you learnt anything recently which throws new light on an earlier piece of work?

- Check grammar, punctuation and spelling. Check also that you have observed the 'rules' of whatever form you are writing in, for example, if it is a letter, that it is addressed and set out correctly.

- Finally, it is a good idea to get a second opinion. Try giving it to a friend to read, or discuss it with your teacher.

Writing

Choose a poem you have written earlier in the course and redraft it following the guidelines given on page 162.

Redraft some of your writing about poetry in the same way.

Over to You

This time it really is 'Over to you', because this is almost the end of the book! However, it is not so much an end as a beginning, because it is only now that you have completed the book that you can study a poem with an appreciation of all its main features. You are now ready to feast at the banquet of English poetry – and to eat GCSE for breakfast!

Diversions

For this final diversion you will need all the skills and knowledge that you have acquired from this book.

Below are tributes to two of England's greatest poets. One of them was written by a very fine poet, and the other with the reputation of being the worst poet in the world. Which is which?

AN ADDRESS TO SHAKESPEARE

Immortal! William Shakespeare, there's none can you excel,
You have drawn out your characters remarkable well,
Which is delightful for to see enacted upon the stage –
For instance, the love-sick Romeo, or Othello, in a rage;
His writings are a treasure, which the world cannot repay,
He was the greatest poet of the past or of the present day –
Also the greatest dramatist, and is worthy of the name,
I'm afraid the world shall never look upon his like again.
His tragedy of Hamlet is moral and sublime,
And for purity of language, nothing can be more fine –
For instance, to hear the fair Ophelia making her moan,
At her father's grave, sad and alone. . . .

In his beautiful play, "As You Like It," one passage is very fine,
Just for instance in the forest of Arden, the language is sublime,
Where Orlando speaks of his Rosalind, most lovely and divine,
And no other poet I am sure has written anything more fine;
His language is spoken in the Church and by the Advocate at the bar,
Here and there and everywhere throughout the world afar;
His writings abound with gospel truths, moral and sublime,
And I'm sure in my opinion they are surpassing fine;
In his beautiful tragedy of Othello, one passage is very fine,
Just for instance where Cassio looses his lieutenancy
... By drinking too much wine;
And in grief he exclaims, "Oh! that men should put an
Enemy in their mouths to steal away their brains."
Immortal! Bard of Avon, your writings are divine,
And will live in the memories of your admirers until the end of time;
Your plays are read in family circles with wonder and delight,
While seated around the fireside on a cold winter's night.

WILLIAM WORDSWORTH

No room for mourning: he's gone out
Into the noisy glen, or stands between the stones
Of the gaunt ridge, or you'll hear his shout
Rolling among the screes, he being a boy again.
He'll never fail nor die
And if they laid his bones
In the wet vaults or iron sarcophagi
Of fame, he'd rise at the first summer rain
And stride across the hills to seek
His rest among the broken lands and clouds.
He was a stormy day, a granite peak
Spearing the sky; and look, about its base
Words flower like crocuses in the hanging woods,
Blank though the dalehead and the bony face.

Can you tell which poem was written by 'the world's worst poet'? Even more important, can you say what is bad about it, and why the other poem is so much better? When you have worked out your answers to these questions, turn to page 166 for comment about both poems, and information about the poets.

Notes on Diversions

Page 44
Did you spot that the whole thing was a spoof? If so, what gave it away?

Below is the 'Spitting Image' version that it was adapted from. Among other faults it shows how repetition can be overdone. What are the 'Spitting Image' team trying to say about today's song-writers?

Write an improved version of the song (if possible!).

Page 57
The poem 'Star Quality' is by the amateur poet. The rhymes in verse one are clumsy. An obvious

opportunity to rhyme 'figure' with 'bigger' has been missed in verse two. Verse three could easily have rhymed with a little rearrangement of words. Instead of 'large group of people' Arthur should have written 'crowd' – it is neater, and it rhymes! We suspect that the shark was only brought in for the sake of rhyme, but this is spoiled by the last line of that verse anyway! There is not much sense of rhythm in the poem, Arthur has just cobbled the words together 'any-old-how'. He is long-winded in making the point of the poem, which is rather trivial and spoilt by big-headedness.

Carl Holman's poem, by comparison, rhymes with consummate ease, the rhymes emphasising key

---

Here are some lyrics sent to me by a budding young lyricist. I have appended my comments (in the red ink) — see if you think they help.

Hi again, Fans. Basically, a fine lyric. I see what our friend is trying to say. Some of the imagery is devastating, and the chorus says it all — although, as I stated, there are probably 46 "Oh yeah's" too many. I would rework this — but do not give up whatever you do.

This is a potential No. 1 lyric, and I'm not just saying that. If you've got talent, don't hide it.

That's what I say.

All the best, Fans. See you soon.

Paul x.

Good rhyme with 'couch'. Unfortunately, should be at the other end of the line for maximum effect. However if 'couch' in line 2 is replaced by 'bed' — you're in the shit. Perhaps you should replace 'head' in line 1 with something that rhymes with 'couch' and 'ouch'. 'Pouch'?

The sun is shining in my head
and I am lying on my couch
Someone hits me on the nose
Ouch I cry, that was sore

BAD. DOESN'T RHYME Just a thought, but you may find 'bed' would be a suitable replacement word here.

Oh yeah, Oh yeah, Oh yeah,
Oh yeah, Oh yeah, Oh yeah
Oh yeah, Oh yeah, Oh yeah
Oh yeah, Oh yeah, Oh yeah
Oh yeah, Oh yeah, Oh yeah

— GOOD

Impressive Vocabulary. There is a suspicion. I'm afraid that you have simply leafed thru the 'M' section of a dictionary

Mash, Mashie, Mask, Mask
Maskar, Maskinonge, Masochism
Mason, Mason-Dixon, Masonry
Masorah, Masorete, Masque

try to keep under the 100 mark.

Oh yeah, Oh yeah, Oh yeah X 146

You could always break it up a bit by spelling 'Yeah' as 'Yeh' on occasion. I think it would help.

My pink toothbrush melts in the purple sun
and seven chocolate horsemen get a
plastic parking ticket

Wow!!

Oh yeah, Oh yeah, Oh yeah.....
(Fade)

Good Idea.

---

words – note particularly how effective this is in the last verse. The rhythm is controlled, and works in harmony with the rhyme, and the subject is interesting and vividly expressed with not a word wasted.

Page 79
The title of the poem is 'Vampire'.

Page 90
This is the 'updated' version of 'While shepherds watched their flocks by night' which appears in *Hymns for Today's Church*:

While shepherds watched their flocks by night
all seated on the ground,
the angel of the Lord came down
and glory shone around.

'Fear not,' said he – for mighty dread
had seized their troubled mind –
'Good news of greatest joy I bring
to you and all mankind.'

'To you in Bethlehem this day
is born of David's line
a saviour, who is Christ the Lord.
And this shall be the sign:

'The heavenly babe you there shall find
to human view displayed,
in simple clothing tightly wrapped
and in a manger laid.'

Thus spoke the seraph, and forthwith
appeared a shining throng
of angels praising God, who thus
addressed their joyful song:

'All glory be to God on high
and to the earth be peace!
To those on whom his favour rests
good will shall never cease.'

N. Tate

Page 113
Julia A Moore fails because the farcical nature of the poem's faults, such as using initials in a name, awkward rhymes, clumsy word order, even bad grammar ('Many ties *was* . . .') make nonsense of its solemn message.

Page 132
Poetry is dying out, and poets have stopped writing, but the everyday misuse of language in the media, advertising, etc., goes on as strongly as ever.

Another point to ponder: why is the poem so much more powerful than the above paraphrase?

Page 163
The second poem was written by Sidney Keyes, a first-rate poet, the first by William McGonnegal, the world's worst poet. McGonnegal's poem is written in what is called doggerel – verse with a monotonous and limping rhythm. His vocabulary is limited – look how often he uses the word 'fine' – and his thought is very superficial. All he basically says is 'this bit is good' and 'that bit is good' with different examples.

Sidney Keyes' poem is skilfully rhymed, the rhymes emphasising the key words in the poem, such as 'hear his *shout*' and 'He'll never fail or *die*'. The poem gets to the heart of Wordsworth's personality – his love of nature, and describes it and his poetry with strikingly appropriate imagery: 'Words flower like crocuses'.

There are four 'bad' poems in this book – the three in these diversions and 'Where is my boy tonight?' on page 108. Which do you think is the worst and why? How do the bad poems help you to appreciate the good ones?

Answers to the riddles on page 97: 'Bookworm' and 'ice'.

Original captions for postcards on page 104:

A 'Waitress! – What does this mean? There is a fly in my cup!!'
'How should I know, I am not a fortune teller!'

B 'If you laid the table, Janet, what about this bad egg?'
'Never laid an egg in my life, Ma'am.'

C 'Take the drawers down first, please!'

Glossary

You will find below an explanation of some of the terms used in this book, and definitions of some of the other terms that you might come across. Limitations of space have meant that this glossary has had to be highly selective. Those who would like more help are referred to *The Dictionary and Handbook of Poetry* by Jack Myers and Michael Simms, which is the most complete guide available.

Alliteration The repetition of consonants or vowels for emphasis or musical effect, for example, '*v*ampires and *v*icars playing *v*iolins in the *v*estry'. See page 97.

Attitude This term is used a number of times in the National Criteria for GCSE. In its fullest sense it is quite a complex term, but it can be understood simply as the writer's feelings towards the subject of the poem. See Chapters 10 and 11.

Ballad A ballad is a story told in verse. Some of the early ballads were passed on by word of mouth and were written down much later. The form became popular again in the nineteenth century, though by this time the oral tradition was dying out.

Blank verse This is the term given to poetry written in a five stress line without rhyme.

Epic A poem of very great length and highly serious subject matter. One of the oldest and greatest epics is the *Iliad* by the Greek poet Homer. The earliest English epic is *Beowulf* by an unknown Anglo–Saxon poet.

Epigram A short, witty poem. An example by Thomas Randolph may be found on page 15.

Epitaph An inscription on a tomb. See page 7.

Figure of speech We often say things that are not literally true for effect: 'she is a tiger when she is angry!' does not mean that she actually turns into a tiger, it is a way of emphasising her anger by using a figure of speech called a **metaphor**; see **Imagery**, **Metaphor** and **Simile**.

Free verse Poetry which is 'free' from strict patterns of rhyme and metre. Look out for a freer use of rhythm, occasional use of rhyme, special use of line layout, repetition, and experimental effects.

Hyperbole This is a figure of speech in which we use exaggeration for effect, for example, 'I've got thousands of friends!'

Imagery The use of word-pictures for vividness of description. The term covers many types of word-picture. Two of the most important are **Simile** and **Metaphor**.

Irony This is saying the opposite of what is meant, for example, if someone broke a plate while helping to wash up, you might say, 'You're a big help!' It also refers to a situation, described in a poem or developed in the plot of a novel, which seems to mock reasonable hopes: 'He died two days before inheriting a fortune.' See Chapter 11.

Jargon Technical terms, especially when they are overused in a way that confuses the ordinary person.

Lyric This means literally 'to be sung to the lyre'. It is used today to mean the words of a song, or a short poem. In a sense it is the opposite of 'epic'.

Metaphor A direct comparison, for example, 'an icy smile'. There are many ways of using metaphors and they can be so interwoven into the language of a poem that it is easy to miss them – look out for things which are not literally true, for example, 'poems are little word machines' is a metaphor because poems are not machines. See **Imagery** and **Simile**.

Metre Metre is the pattern of stressed and unstressed syllables in a line of poetry (see **Rhythm**). To analyse the metre of a line of poetry, first read it slowly and emphatically, listening for the stressed syllables, and mark them in with a diagonal stroke. Mark in the unstressed syllables with a cross, and then study the pattern (if the pattern is irregular then the poem is not metrical). The two commonest patterns are:

✕ ╱ ✕   ╱ ✕ ╱✕ ╱ ✕ ╱
Shall I compare thee to a summer's day?

This is IAMBIC metre – unstressed followed by stressed syllable.

╱ ✗ ╱ ✗ ╱✗ ╱✗

Shall I take you to a disco?

This is a TROCHAIC metre – stressed followed by unstressed syllable.

There are others. If you wish to study the subject in more detail see *The Poets' Manual and Rhyming Dictionary* by Frances Stillman.

Onomatopoeia Occurs when a word echoes the sound of the thing it describes, for example, 'buzz', 'splash', etc. See page 101.

Parody A humorous imitation.

Pun A play on the double meaning of a word, for example, 'Is a vicar's budgie a bird of pray?' See page 92.

Refrain A line, or a number of lines, which is regularly repeated at the end of each verse. In songs, it is called the 'chorus'. See page 43 for an example.

Rondeau A poem fifteen lines rhymed *a a b b a a a b (refrain) a a b b a (refrain)*. These poems are very difficult to write because only two rhymes are used throughout the whole poem. See **Rhyme**.

Rhyme Two words ending with the same sound are said to rhyme. **Rhyme-schemes** are notated by using letters of the alphabet – '*a*' for the first word, and any other word that rhymes with it, '*b*' for the second and so on:

I love the way he smiles at me,	*a*
I love the way he calls me 'honey',	*b*
But what thrills me with ecstasy	*a*
Is spending all his lovely money!	*b*

The rhyme-scheme is *a b a b*.

Rhythm Not to be confused with metre. Rhythm is the use of the stress, weight and even the length of sounds for various effects – creating a smooth flow of words, emphasis, contrast, or to echo the meaning. Often the effects of rhythm and metre are played off against each other. See page 60.

Sarcasm Bitterness, especially when ironically worded.

Simile A comparison, or word-picture, using the words 'like' or 'as', for example, 'She smiled at me, a smile like ice.' See **Imagery** and **Metaphor**.

Sonnet One of the most popular of set forms. It has fourteen five-stress lines. Many different rhyme-schemes are possible.

Stanza Another word for a verse of a poem.

Syllable A sound produced by a single effort of the voice, for example, 'drink' has one syllable, 'bouncer' two syllables, and 'discotheque' has three syllables.

Synonyms Words of similar meaning. Very few synonyms have exactly the same shade of meaning. Note that a thesaurus lists synonyms and a dictionary gives definitions.

Villanelle This is one of the most difficult rhyming forms. There are six verses but only two rhymes throughout. An added difficulty is that the first and third lines of the first verse are used as refrains. The rhyme-scheme is (numbers refer to refrains): $A^1 b A^2$ $a b A^1$ $a b A^2$ $a b A^1$ $a b A^2$ $a b A^1 A^2$. Before trying to write one of your own, it would be wise to study an example of the form.

Teacher's Notes

This book, and my own teaching of poetry, is based on three main principles which are given below in the hope that they may be found helpful.

- **Poetry is language at its most exciting.** Any attempt to teach poetry which does not convey that excitement will ultimately fail. GCSE, by making poetry a compulsory element of literature courses, has ensured that it receives the attention it deserves. However, though the syllabuses encourage lively and innovative approaches, there is a danger that anxieties about the examination, especially the requirement to write about a previously unseen poem, may inhibit lively teaching. My sincere conviction is that if pupils enjoy their poetry lessons, the examination will look after itself.

- **Poetry is part of life.** In the broadest sense of the word, poetry can be found everywhere, from pupils' own speech to the lyrics of pop songs. In the more specific sense, poetry is about life, and grows out of life. To feel this for themselves, pupils need to read poems about things which concern them, written in a style they can relate to. Matching poem to pupil is one of the most challenging of the teacher's tasks – and one of the most rewarding. If pupils can feel the relevance of poetry to their lives, they will take away with them much more than a GCSE certificate!

- **Poetry should be studied as poetry.** Poems may be interesting for their content, and may provide valuable illustrations of a theme, but unless attention is given to the way the content is expressed, the essence of poetry is missed. In poetry the medium is the message, as this excellent definition from a *Dictionary and Handbook of Poetry* by Jack Myers and Michael Simms makes clear:

poem (*from Greek for 'thing created'*) *an artistically organised use of language that cannot be replaced by PARAPHRASE. Generally speaking, a poem will use all or some of the*

following: RHYTHM, IMAGERY, SONICS, RHETORICAL AND POETICAL DEVICES, TYPOGRAPHICAL ARRANGEMENT, selective DICTION, economical PHRASING, LINE ENDING, and qualities of imagination, emotion, and insightfulness . . .

This goes far beyond the requirements of the GCSE subject criteria, and all these features are covered, in more or less detail, in this book.

How to Use This Book

Pen Rhythms is addressed to the pupil, making it suitable for individual and group work. Each chapter begins with a simple explanation followed by poems and other materials, and continues with an 'Over to You' section which contains suggestions for activities and written work. This leaves the teacher free to circulate, join in discussions and give advice and guidance as appropriate.

The needs of a broad ability range are catered for by keeping explanations simple, but these are supplemented by a glossary which contains information of a more technical kind for those pupils who are interested.

Most chapters are self-contained, allowing the book to be used flexibly: dipped into for ideas, integrated with English language work, or used as an anthology.

The book can be followed as a coursebook. Pupils who work through this book will have covered all the aspects of poetry mentioned in the above definition and much more besides. Chapter 15 brings together these various aspects of poetry and shows how they can be applied in different ways to the study of a poet or a theme. There are also suggestions for a wide range of imaginative responses to poetry and tips for redrafting work. For this reason it would be a good idea to dip into this chapter while working through the book. For example, it could be particularly useful to draw pupils' attention to the imaginative responses on page 161.

The 'Diversions' which end each chapter reinforce both the point of the chapter and the general message that poetry is enjoyable. They can be used as worthwhile 'fillers' for odd moments in lessons.

Throughout the book pupils are encouraged to write their own poems, as this is the best way for pupils to develop an understanding and appreciation of the poems they read.

The subject 'English' is an indivisible whole, therefore every opportunity should be taken to integrate work on poetry with other aspects of the subject. There are many points in this book which could be used as a basis for related work in English language or spoken English: the poems about advertising and journalism, for example, or the chapters on the use of words.

This book is particularly effective when used as a 'core' alongside a range of anthologies and other poetry books. Techniques, themes and the work of individual poets can then be explored more fully. Some suggested titles are given below.

Bibliography

For teachers who wish to brush up on their own knowledge of poetry, the following books are particularly recommended:

Geoffrey Leech, *A Linguistic Guide to English Poetry* (Longman, 1969)

Jack Myers and Michael Simms, *The Dictionary and Handbook of Poetry* (Longman, 1985)

Frances Stillman, *A Poet's Manual and Rhyming Dictionary* (Thames & Hudson, 1966)

Peter Tunnicliffe, *Poetry Experience* (Methuen, 1984)

Teaching Poetry in the Secondary School: An HMI view (HMSO, 1987)

Most English departments already have a large stock of anthologies which could be used alongside this book. Dig deep: some very old and dusty ones could have just as much to offer as the latest publications. Among recently published anthologies I have found the following particularly useful:

Martin Booth (ed.), *British and North American Contemporary Verse* (Oxford University Press, 1981) – arranged by poet

Stewart Brown (ed.), *Caribbean Poetry Now* (Hodder and Stoughton, 1984) – arranged by theme

F E S Finn (ed.), *Voices of Today: An anthology of recent verse* (John Murray, 1980) – arranged by theme

Geoffrey Halson (ed.), *Interactions: A poetry teaching anthology* (Longman, 1982) – arranged by theme

Michael Harrison and Christopher Stuart-Clarke (eds.), Narrative Poems (Oxford University Press, 1981)

Jack Hydes (ed.), *Touched With Fire* (Cambridge University Press, 1985) – an anthology ranging over the past 400 years

George Macbeth (ed.), *Poetry for Today* (Longman, 1984) – arranged by poet

Index of Authors

171

Text © Chris Webster 1988
Original line artwork © Stanley Thornes (Publishers) Ltd 1988

First published in 1988 by:
Stanley Thornes (Publishers) Ltd
Old Station Drive
Leckhampton
CHELTENHAM GL53 0DN
England

British Library Cataloguing in Publication Data

Webster, C. (Christopher)
    Pen rhythms.
    1. Poetry – For schools
    I. Title
    808.1

ISBN 0–85950–837–4

Typeset by Tech-Set, Tyne & Wear.
Printed and bound in Great Britain at The Bath Press, Avon.